THROUGH SALT SPRAYED EYES

By ROBERT WELSH
Radio Officer, Merchant Navy.

Acknowledgement

I am indebted to my sister in law, Elizabeth Melville, as proof reader and self confessed pedagogue for applying her talents and unstinted time to my "Magnum opus navalis." Cliches and peppered punctuation have been scuttled or sailed through to render my script more acceptable for which I express my sincere thanks.

i

PREFACE

When he was eighteen years of age my son returned home one evening having been chatting with his colleagues as they discussed their fathers' lives in World War Two. His immediate reaction was to ask me, "Were you in the War, father?" This was the stimulus to encourage me to write about my experiences believing that they will perhaps answer his questions, knowing that until now they have lain silently buried with the past.

My invitation to the service commemorating the 50th anniversary of the Battle of the Atlantic further suggested that members of the Merchant Navy who died should be remembered and those of us who were fortunate to survive should make others aware of the sacrifices that they made.

The Flag Officer Plymouth
requests the pleasure of your company
at the

50th Anniversary of the Battle of the Atlantic
to be held at Liverpool Cathedral
on Sunday, 30th May, 1993 at 10.30 a.m.

R.S.V.P.
The Commanding Officer
HMS EAGLET
Princes Dock
Liverpool L3 0AA

This invitation will not
gain you admission to the Cathedral,
admission tickets will be issued
on 1st May, 1993

THE MERCHANT NAVY.

Have you stood on the bridge at midnight?
Not the bridge o'er the purling stream,
But the bridge of an old tramp steamer
Deep laden and broad of beam.

Have you peered far into the darkness?
With rain blind and salt sprayed eyes
And cursed the luck that brought you
To race for so poor a prize.

Have you stood in the dimly lit wheel house,
Eyes on the lubber mark,
As she moved away crab fashion
And you swore that she steered like the ark?

Have you ever watched for the lighthouse
With its cheerful comforting rays
Telling you of the good shot you'd made
Without a sight for days?

Have you stumbled around in the galley,
Stove top full of sliding pans
And swear your seven bell breakfast
Would be in the also- rans?

Have you ever been in the stokehold
With its fierce and fiery glow
When the Second shouted, "More steam!"
If you stopped, those engines must go.

If you have, then you'll know the meaning
Of the story I try to tell
Of the men who leave home and comfort
For a form of modified hell.

It isn't all plain sailing
O'er calm and sunny seas
Lying in fancy deck chairs
And fanned by a gentle breeze.

Why they sweat to the bones in the tropics
And freeze to the core in the poles
And brave those angry combers
Which are hungry for human souls.

When the storm makes your windows rattle
And you curse when you cannot sleep
Do you ever think of those sailormen
Out there on the rolling deep?

While the only thing that divides them
From all eternity
Is the skill and the strength of that frail iron shell
And faith in the God of the sea.

Now here's a thing to remember
Something you always should do
When you say grace for the food that you get
Thank God- but give sailors their due.

Anon.

CONTENTS

1

STORM AND ATLANTIC BATTLE

THE SPELL OF THE SEA

Britain has always had a maritime culture. Throughout the early part of this 20th Century, we had the largest fleet of merchant ships in the world. Over 50% of world trade was handled by ships flying the Red Ensign. Indeed when one reflects upon our maritime heritage we remember that we are a nation of seafarers. Furthermore, we are an island race and have the longest coastline in Europe. From most parts of Britain the sea can be reached within the hour. It seems entirely appropriate, therefore, that I should feel the call of the sea.

In my youth, all our great rivers bristled with shipping as vessels bustled in and out of the docks with cargoes from every corner of the globe. Even in city parks gentlemen could be seen with their model yachts enjoying racing on the large public ponds. The popular class of "10-Raters" were sleek sailboats almost six feet long and spectators could indulge in imaginary on board experiences, as the boats rippled across the lake. From a distance they seemed replicas in miniature, of those magnificent "J Class" yachts with their tall 80ft masts elegantly carrying 15,000 sq.ft. of sail. Sir Thomas Lipton's "Shamrock" and Sir Thomas Sopwith's "Endeavour," were both challengers for the Americas` Cup. I watched these fantastic "J Class" craft racing around our coast at the peak of yacht racing history and probably also the peak of extravagance in pleasure sailing. As a schoolboy, these mental images were the infection which inevitably cultivated my sea fever. At school, John Masefield's "Sea Fever" further fostered the frenetic infection.

I must go down to the seas again, to the lonely sea and the sky,
And all I ask is a tall ship and a star to steer her by,
And the wheel's kick and the wind's song
and the white sail's shaking,
And a grey mist on the sea's face and a grey dawn breaking...

John Masefield enticed me to sea even under engine. Evocative imagery inspired me in the last verse of his "Cargoes."

Dirty British coaster with a salt caked smoke stack
Butting through the Channel in the mad March days,
With a cargo of Tyne coal,
Road rail, pig lead,
Firewood, iron ware, and cheap tin trays.

My aspirations surged aboard that coaster; I could feel the thrust of her bluff bow butting through the waves. My conscience said "Must do!" and so I pressed the button "Enter" into memory.

As children, we enjoyed our summer holidays sailing around the islands and lochs of the Clyde estuary. This of course was the birth place of the world's first commercial steam ship. Henry Bell, of Helensburgh, launched his little wooden paddle steam boat "Comet" in 1812, which started the World's first advertised commercial operation of a steamship and the "doon the watter" sailings.

It is interesting that the ship's bridge, the brain of every vessel, gets its name from the bridge-like structure which straddled the paddle boxes of the early steamers. The master could thus more easily move from one side to the other to control the vessel in confined waters. The elevated position gave the best all round view and soon steering was operated from the bridge. Control of the ship no longer required a position astern from which to view the sails.

Clyde steamers had 118 piers available as landing stages from which passengers could alight. As many as thirty steamers per day left Glasgow and regular hourly services between ports of call meant that we could spend our summer months "doon the watter" enjoying these sailing opportunities!

Boat handling skills also were honed to perfection as we busied ourselves on rowing boats or motor boats launched from the shore at **Largs.** How sad it is to observe that today, all these facilities have virtually vanished. Summer months could not have provided a happier or more rewarding childhood than our salty germination. On 26th September1935, No.534 was launched from John Brown's shipyard and christened **"Queen Mary."** She was over 1,000 feet long and had to be launched at an angle up the river Clyde in order to accommodate her tremendous length. The stern was directed into the mouth of the River Cart to make available this extra sea-room at the opposite bank. That is where I was standing to watch the launch of the greatest ship the world had ever seen. I had to run backwards as she pushed the wash with her stern across the river. I was twelve years old and just escaped a ducking. I never dreamt that one day I would sail on her and risk another ducking. Likewise I had no idea that within four years we would be at war.

ANSWERING THE CALL
Call up was approaching and I had a good friend in David Stenhouse. He was sixteen years of age. David had been to sea in the Merchant Navy as an apprentice navigation officer. After his first voyage, his parents brought him ashore, saying, "When you are old enough, David, you will do your duty, but meantime enjoy family life while you can." The perils of the sea in wartime startled everyone ashore and nobody would dispute that it was neither the time nor the place for a lad so young. Eventually, David did answer his country's call and returned to sea a month before "D.Day." Sadly, he was lost in that operation. It was David who told me that the Radio Officer had the best job on the ship. He wore a smart uniform and was completely independent of the

workings of the ship and the rest of the crew. He was responsible to the Captain only for the operation of the wireless room and when in port, free to come and go as he pleased. That was the "jam" but there was no mention of any flies. On the other hand, my friend and next door neighbour joined the Merchant Navy as a Radio Officer. He ventured forth the year ahead of me but within his first week at sea the ship was sunk and he perished. This episode, together with other known losses, meant that little was left to the imagination about the perils of the sea.

I was aware that in the normal course of "Call Up," stating a preference for the Royal Navy meant little and I could be drafted into the Army or Air force depending upon the luck of the draw. I volunteered to go to sea in the Merchant Navy before I would be required by the Services. There was a desperate shortage of Radio Officers in the Merchant Navy. Sometimes they were referred to as the R\O, wireless operator or affectionately addressed as "Sparks." The medical examination was cursory because of the shortage of trained operators and our longevity was uncertain. A watch was held to my ear."Can you hear that?" Well, one had to be daft to say, "no!"

I attended a Wireless College for which I had to pay all expenses until I had acquired the ability to read Morse at the speed of sixteen characters per second. Normally, the college training would require a period of one year or more. Wartime exigences reduced this to six months. Since I was paying my own expenses, I opted to attend the evening training sessions as well, but at no extra cost! This twelve hour daily stint enabled me to qualify in only three months. This achievement was a record for the college and I was acknowledged as the fastest ever to qualify. A certificate of proficiency in radiotelegraphy was granted by the Postmaster General and qualified me to join the Marconi International Marine Communication Company. Now, the appeal for adventure, responsibility, independence and a nomadic existence, was about to be fulfilled. As happens, adventure and excitement is closer to disaster than one anticipates.

Most shipowners leased the radio equipment and the services of the Radio Officers from the appropriate company. The Marconi International Marine Communication Company was the biggest. I never knew to what type of ship or part of the world I was destined. A short trip perhaps to Canada and back would result in three days leave. Docking at London, for example, I would sign off straight away, then nip up home to Glasgow. In wartime, under blackout conditions, the train would be halted intermittently. Numerous hold-ups, air raid threats and shuddering halts meant that the journey was interminable. But the discomfort of twenty hours packed like sardines in the corridor of a blacked out train, simply vanished at the thought that the delightful destination was home. The train was packed with uniformed servicemen and although we were tired and weary, there were always jovial overtones.

The second day at home the telegraph boy, on his red push bike, would hand me the telegram to report the following day at Liverpool, Newcastle, or perhaps London. We never faltered. This was in effect, volunteering every trip. I did know of one R/O attached to the *Queen Mary* with all its attendant protocol. He had accrued fourteen days leave. After one week he was recalled but declined, saying that he wanted his further week's leave. When he did report, he found himself mounting the gangway of a rusty old tramp steamer. The captain seeing "Sparks" in his Great Coat of Admiral appearance asked, "A punishment job, is it?"

In 1840 Samuel Morse devised his code as a means of communication along American railroads between stations. The first ship to be fitted with a commercial wireless station was in 1900. After the "Titanic" disaster, all ocean going ships had to install Radio so that help could be summoned beyond the visual area. The system of dots and dashes could then be used to communicate with other ships and even to the land stations. During the war, three Radio

5

Officers were required on each ship in order to maintain twenty-four hours' continuous radio watch.

GUNNERY COURSE

I was asked if I would be prepared to take the Merchant Navy Gunnery Course. " Certainly!" I replied. Thus in early 1942 I had completed a course which qualified me in firing and the maintenance of Hotchkiss and Marlin machine guns. The appropriate certificate was duly awarded. I had to admire the bravery of the Fleet Air Arm pilot who flew across the firing range, towing a long sock behind his plane. We novices, taking doubtful aim at it, enjoyed the practice. Sometimes over enthusiasm had released live rounds which hit the plane, but not often!

VISUAL SIGNALLING COURSE

Because one can decipher dots and dashes at high speed does not mean that one can interpret messages visually signalled by light. Wireless telegraphy is a rhythmic series of sounds bearing almost no relationship to silent flashes of light. Some Radio operators are out of their depth if required to read visual signals. I had no intention of lacking on that account. Thus I volunteered to take the visual signalling course which resulted in a certificate of proficiency. Confidently, I took on the responsibility to read Morse by light whenever the occasion warranted. This was a great boost to morale for a teenage sailor helping out on the bridge. This qualification was particularly appropriate on a Danish ship, where language compounded Morse reading difficulties.

SS.NORDLYS

The Danish ship ss.Nordlys came under British control, in April 1940, when the invasion of Denmark took place. The ship was intercepted by the Royal Navy off Aalesand, and taken to Kirkwall. As the Danish Government surrendered to Germany and did not have a Government in exile - as did Norway and Holland. - any Danish ships which fell into British hands were transferred to the British flag. Thus, the "Nordlys" became a British ship for the du-

MERCHANT NAVY A/A GUNNERY COURSE.

CERTIFICATE OF PROFICIENCY.

GLASGOW 9th May 1942.

No. 3422.

Naval Army or Training Centre

Name........ R. WELSH.

Rank or Rating........ Radio.

B. of T. or D.B. No........

has completed the Merchant Navy A/A Gunnery

Course and is qualified in the firing and

cleaning and oiling of a,

.... Hotchkiss and Marlin.

machine gun.

Rank........

D.E.M.S.
Training Centre. GLASGOW

VALID FOR 4 MONTHS ONLY,
RE-QUALIFICATION THEN NECESSARY.

Radio Officers

of the

Merchant Navy

Visual Signalling Course

Certificate of
Proficiency

Third Radio Officer I am in my
teens but the ferocious Atlantic
and the merciless times were to
mould a meaningful maturity.

ration and was put under the management of W.A.Massey & Sons, Hull. She was built in 1916 by the Copenhagen shipyard of Burmeister & Wain. This company still builds ships and diesel engines. The Norden Steamship company has a long history, being founded in 1871 and is still in business. Each ship carried "Nord.."as part of its name. The "Nordlys" (Northern Lights) was 4000 tons grt. and designed primarily for the Scandinavian coast and the Baltic. She did not have a raised fo'c's'le which would have been more weatherly thus offering more protection against the winter storms of the North Atlantic.

I joined the *ss.Nordlys* in London. I was duly impressed that the Danish crew had courageously volunteered to continue sailing in dangerous times. They could so easily have opted out. Members of other countries in similar circumstances had been neither cooperative nor courageous and in effect had become antagonistic.

Leaving London, we sailed up the East coast and round to Loch Ewe on the North West tip of Scotland where ships gathered in readiness to join their Atlantic convoys. As we entered the loch, the early hours of darkness shaded the remaining wintery daylight. Surrounding lochside hills seemed dark and foreboding and the vitreous black ebony of the loch's surface inspired thoughts of "still waters run deep." The sheltered position of Loch Ewe, almost hidden by those awesome steep hills and its great depth were, of course, the attributes which determined its war time role. It was a safe haven. Outside were the misty islands. The whole of that Hebridean area captured my imagination. It seemed mystical with a magic which enticed me to write home promising that one day I would be sailing to enjoy the romance and beauty of this coast.

The hour of departure came and we slipped out into the Atlantic to meet with our appointed convoy which was sailing northwards from England.The main section would have departed from Liverpool. Gathering all the ships together in correct formation was a remarkable planning and navigational operation. Each ship flew the numerical flags representing her designated position. Thus

9

No.54 would indicate the fourth ship in column five of the convoy.

It soon became obvious that our course was directed much further north than usual as we struggled to avoid the U.Boats. I saw that there was a large amount of plankton in the seas clearly indicating that we were in Icelandic waters. These tiny creatures are quite re-markable in their effect. When the sea crashed overboard at night, every single bubble of foam was illuminated as it radiated a phos-phorescent glow. It looked like a whole series of little light bulbs flowing along the deck to cascade out of the scuppers in a tum-bling luminous dash. Wherever there was foam, its fantastical ef-fects were phosphorescent. Even the ship's bow wave at night emitted a dazzling glare visible over quite a distance. Wave crests appeared as bright glowing beams of light tumbling and flashing as they rolled over. This truly was an exhibition of nature's ability to amaze. Plankton are tiny creatures which transform the appear-ance of the sea into a luminiferous display of phosphorescent pyrotechnics, unparalleled anywhere ashore.

AURORA BOREALIS. (Northern Lights).
Nature, however, was still capable of working magic on a grander scale. Fortunately, it was close to the Spring Equinox, when the Aurora can be seen at its best. The further north one travels the greater the spectacle. It is just unbelievable to witness this display of atmospheric lights, peculiar to these northern high latitudes. A series of heavenly search lights of variable colours diffuse across the sky from the horizon. Halos project bands of light which drift across the heavens swirling in a kaleidoscope of colours and shapes. It is a breathtaking, changing display of atmospheric shafts and flashes of lights caused by electrical discharges in the atmosphere. The Aurora occurs when the Earth's magnetic field interacts with the solar wind, a gust of charged particles streaming from the sun. In the radio room the atmospheric ghosting of sig-nals on the wireless was unusually pronounced because of these magnetic effects.

Perhaps the name of a ship is an imaginative reflection of a sailor's dream. In these northern waters, we were basking in the lume of the Aurora. How appropriate to sail through a dream and be entranced by the spectacle of the Northern Lights on board this ship, the *Nordlys*. There are those who might be *Dreaming of a White Christmas just like the ones they used to know.* Similarly, fond memories of the *heavenly dancers* inspire Aberdonians to sing *The Northern Lights of Old Aberdeen mean Home Sweet Home to me.* The spectacle is most pronounced and familiar to those of us living in the northern part of Britain. To the seafarer it is all part of life as he enjoys nature intensified and magnified beyond anything witnessed ashore. She unfolds countless awe inspiring displays, both in the heavens and with her wonders of the deep. The description of a ship in a storm by the psalmist reflects on these matters. In Psalm 107 the psalmist writes.

> They that go down to the sea in ships, that do business in great waters;
> these see the works of the Lord, and his wonders in the deep.
> For he commandeth and raiseth the stormy wind,
> which lifteth up the waves thereof.
> They mount up to the heaven, they go down again to the depths;
> their soul is melted because of trouble.
> They reel to and fro, and stagger like a drunken man,
> and are at their wit's end.
> Then they cry unto the Lord in their trouble,
> and he bringeth them out of their distresses.
> He maketh the storm a calm, so that the waves thereof are still.
> Then are they glad because they be quiet;
> so he bringeth them unto their desired haven.

War imposes limitations to this peaceful outcome. Suddenly and silently in the dead of night a torpedo might open up watery graves. The first sinking may catch the escorts unaware, merely announcing that there is menace lurking in the surrounding black depths. This convoy was no exception, though without further research, I cannot say authoritatively, how many ships we lost. It is suffice to confirm that night after night we came under horrendous attacks with unceasing ferocity. I recall at one stage, after days followed by nights of unremitting anguish and mental torture, that I found myself thinking that it might be better if we were to be bumped. This would overcome a situation against which we had no defence. It would be a release from our suffering, frustration and the inability to make any response. At least I could then strive to survive.

Thinking this way opened an awareness of the enormity of first having to escape from the explosion, of then taking on those mountainous seas, in the middle of the night, under icy temperatures and biting winds. These were frightening factors for contemplation. Upon reflection I realised that I was relatively comfortable and dry. Absent was the soaking wet torture expected in arctic conditions whilst floating in those mountainous seas. The conclusion, therefore, was that the U.Boats could continue to do their damnedest whilst I resigned myself with fortitude to passively resist their skulking threats. With grim determination we obdurately battled on, doggedly refusing to be ready victims. It was satisfying, knowing that as we survived we were thus evolving as victors.

Because of language obstacles, much of my time was spent on the bridge assisting with signalling, either by Morse or flags. The cold was unbelievable. Only by piling on layers of woollen clothing and then finishing off with a hooded duffel coat could I endure my spell out on the bridge. I credit this coat with my survival. The bitter wind with blast freezing intensity hurled itself around me intent upon biting through all clothing and solidifying me into a pinnacle of solid ice where I stood. The salt spray formed icicles on the surface of the duffel coat but that was the outer layer. Within its protective fabric my vital forces still flowed. The coat was windproof and the hood in particular helped thwart the icy blast provided I looked in the opposite direction. It was an incredible ship's garment, which we three Radio Officers shared as we took our turn of watch on the bridge in the bitter onslaught.
STORM
The weather during these early winter months has been recorded as

the worst of the century. In a previous convoy the Commodore's ship turned over and immediately vanished. It was overpowered by the might of the ocean and enemy action was not suspected. A following convoy lost a trawler, victim to the storms. The uncontrollable forces of nature if reaching the maximum storm have been shown in tests that these wind-driven waves can technically reach a height of 190 feet. This is an awesome thought which hovers to haunt one when hearing screaming 100-mile-an-hour winds and tumultuous ninety-foot seas. The fact that we took twenty-two days to cross from Loch Ewe to Halifax demonstrates that we were stalled time and again. We had to adopt survival tactics on more than one occasion.

This length of passage could be covered by the *Queen Mary* in merely four days. On the return journey we covered the distance in sixteen days. Hurricane winds and sixty foot waves were encountered for days on end. It was atrocious weather with intermittent blizzards in a biting wind whose knife-sharp edge cut cold to the skin.

Standing on the bridge which is forty feet above the sea we still had to look upwards to watch a mighty advancing wall of water, its curling crest rolling and tumbling towards us. It was a menacing sight to witness its approach. From a position towering several feet above it came crashing closer. This is an awesome situation just a few heart beats away from eternity. Is it possible that the ship could actually mount that staggeringly high rolling mass of sea? Then the gallant ship with bow burying into the wall, shudders, shakes and with her buoyancy lifting her forward section she rises ponderously, slowly, upwards, until almost reaching the top of the wave. Then the effort seems too much and several tons of ocean cascade from the top of the crest to come pounding on board. The crashing sea breaks over the fo'csle and rushes headlong down the deck tumbling and foaming out of the scuppers. The tremendous extra weight of water on deck makes the ship's movements sluggish and agonisingly slow as she struggles to free herself. Such swamping by tons of water, makes one realise that if it had crashed on to the hatch top of number one hold, this could have been stove in. That would then have been the end of the story. Making its way to the top of the wave the ship reaches forward and beyond the crest. The bow section now moves clear out of water and into the air. The wave continues to pass along under the length of the hull until only the middle section of the ship is supported by the sea. Momentarily, suspended on the top of the crest, this is a backbreaking position. Ships loaded with heavy cargoes such as iron ore, do not tolerate this situation for long. Fortunately, ours was *light* ship with only minimum ballast.

The moment now comes for the white knuckle drop. It is similar to falling down a forty foot lift shaft and one becomes weightless. The bow, momentarily poised on the crest of the wave has advanced just far enough to become front heavy. It falls through the air, downwards all forty feet or more until it reaches the bottom. The momentum and the final crash defies description. Surely this impact is beyond the limits of tolerance and endurance of any ship. A few hovering seconds of impending doom follow as one awaits to discover if the forepart is still intact and not split open. Is our bluff bow capable of rising yet again out of the deep hollow? It is not unknown for ships at this stage to continue to drive downwards into the oncoming wave and disappear into the ocean. A thought that is not easily dispelled.

Fortunately, she is starting the long lift up the face of the next wave. Because her stern is now pointing high in the air out of water, her propeller is free to rotate violently without any drag. Whirling round, its heavy weight causes the entire ship to shake and vibrate from stem to stern. Thus she shudders and shakes her way up the next oncoming wave, easing vibrations only when the propeller is next submerged. This is repeated hour after hour, damage mounts, plates split, rivets shake loose, but amazingly these sound vessels have a will to survive.

Combating the weather does have its consequences. Several ships unable to cope with the hurricane winds and formidable seas, dropped out astern of the convoy. These stragglers were, however, fortunate that the seas were too rough for submarines to surface and torpedo with any degree of accuracy. When the weather abated these ships steamed full ahead and eventually caught up to reclaim their positions. We ourselves suffered damage to our steering gear. The violent pressures on the rudder put too much strain on the steering linkage. Breaking down left us with a nervous situation. Everyone suddenly became alert knowing that when you become a straggler and isolated you become most vulnerable. Until we could rejoin the convoy we would float alone and offer our predators a stationary target. These pressures no doubt motivated the engineers to effect a speedy repair. All credit must go to them because we were under way again before the convoy could disappear from view.

Naturally, some of the crew became upset with the incessant surges upwards and the dropping downwards through space which the severe weather meted out. Sea sickness is unpleasant but two members of the DEMS group became seriously ill. Defensively Equipped Merchant Ships had old naval guns which were manned and maintained by Royal Navy personnel. These two chaps continued with seasickness to the distressing stage when they were retching blood. At Halifax they were put ashore to recover and would be likely to avoid further seagoing. I succumbed to seasickness for a couple of days until becoming acclimatised to the exceptional circumstances. At home as a child I was renowned for not being quick enough to reach the bathroom. Whilst asleep with my brother I have been chastised for jettisoning my offensive stomach contents upon his person. Brothers do not have a sense of humour in these circumstances. With brother in mind I included this little snip of humour in my letter home.

THE ODE TO THE PAIL

Our Bert is in the navy now,
He's off to sea, you know,
And everywhere our Bertie treads
A bucket's sure to go.

You'll see him if he's up on watch,
It sits there in the corner,
And ere a minute passes
He lets it have a stormer.

His cheeks are fine and rosy now,
But watch them change their hue,
They'll fade through red to yellow,
And then you'll see him spew.

I'll just give you this warning
In case you do not know.
It's "Stand Clear, Everybody!"
For Bert just lets it go.

And if by chance you are not quick
When Bert is on the job,
As sure as fate you'll get it
As sure as Bert is Bob.
I must say, though, as time went on
Our Bertie soon got better
And as the salt got in his blood
He soon became much fitter.

No more is it an ordeal
For Bertie under sail,
He marches up and down the deck
Without that dreadful pail.

-oOo-

Danish cuisine provided an incentive to regain interest in food. It was different possibly because of the presentation and combination of ingredients. Herrings are familiar Scottish fare but breakfasting on raw salt herrings with raw onion slices is the Danish equivalent. Likewise a fruit soup was novel because of its combinations, whilst their beetroot soup did surprise my taste buds. The bread was wonderful and varied, with delights which a good appetite could relish. The coffee, on the otherhand, detracted from an over-all menu of complete satisfaction. All day long a large kettle simmered away on top of the stove. It contained the ground coffee which was continously being topped up during the day, until there was insufficient space for the water. Consequently a full strength aromatic stimulant was produced but it would require more time than I was likely to spare to acquire its taste. It was drunk black, very, very black!

In the officers' dining saloon the conversation of the Danes provided the chief Sparks and myself with much amusement. We enjoyed the absurdity of trying to guess the trend and topic of conversation. Until suddenly a joke or humorous remark provoked loud laughter around the table. This was infectious and we found ourselves in the ludicrous situation of boisterously laughing with their merriment whilst not understanding the reason. It was hilarious fun and besides, talking was no problem. If we initiated a conversation, they kindly responded in their best English.

Fog and ice were expected, but icebergs, magnificent as they appeared, caused shivers of surprise. We arrived amongst them as we approached the Newfoundland Grand Banks. These bergs drift down with the Labrador current. Naturally, they are a danger to shipping but they are truly spectacular. We tinkled our way through floating ice cubes in the Atlantic cocktail as the first berg ghosted out of the fog. One cannot ignore the fact that the mountainous iceberg reveals only one ninth of its terror. This one was brilliant and a really magnificent sight, which dwarfed our ship.

Little wonder that ice patrols now alert shipping with ice conditions and the positions of drifting icebergs.One convoy, diverted to avoid a wulf pack, lost several ships which tangled too close with a group of bergs. Our experience in the ice was not to be missed but we were happy that we did miss that iceberg.

HALIFAX

Entering Halifax Bay we dropped anchor in the shelter of Bedford Basin. " Finished with engines" was rung on the bridge telegraph. The rhythmic throb and heart beat of the ship stopped. The steady pulsations of the engines ceased. Immediately, the quiet was overwhelming. The ship lay motionless on a tranquil inlet. There was complete and utter stillness. Morning was emerging with mist rising from the bay and slowly drifting across the surface. A hazy sense of peace distilled a spellbinding serenity. Those angry hostile seas we had just left behind, heightened the contrasts with our new world. Eyes scanned the scenic shore, fascinated with the wonder of this strange land. Tall fir trees with log cabins cradled amongst the wooded hills proclaimed, it was Canada. In the distance, a woodburning steam train blew its whistle. The sound panted out in delightful outbursts immediately identifiable as a Canadian Railway. The engine laboured gainfully to pull an apparently endless line of trucks only disappearing around a bend into the trees after I had counted the first fifty.

AMMUNITION SHIP

Excitement on board was mounting as we speculated on how soon we might go ashore. Likewise anticipation electrified our desire to move alongside. The experienced hands dropped hints about what could be expected when we stepped ashore. Strangely, one of the first stories circulating was that Halifax had been blown asunder by an ammunition ship. It exploded in the harbour and all who heard the tale were awe-struck by the devastation and havoc that followed from the blast. Several houses disappeared completely and the town never quite recovered from the shock. It was odd, because later I discovered that the explosion had happened many

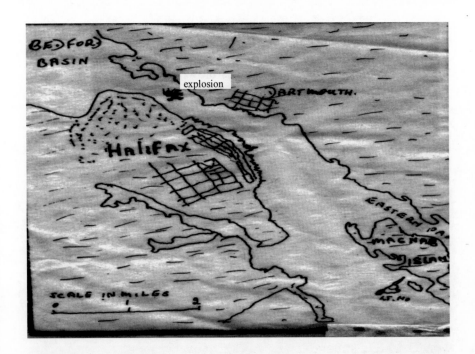

years before and thus seemed just oral history. Surely, it was hardly relevant to recount this tale, even if it had highlighted the past. Its relevance soon became apparent, as I learned that we were about to become an *ammunition ship.* We were destined to move alongside and to load up with explosives.

I had experienced the Luftwaffe dropping their bombs to devastate our docks and cities at home but what they wrought over several air raids could happen **in seconds** when an ammunition ship is blown up. It was on December 6, 1917 that the French freighter the *Mont Blanc* and the Norwegian cargo vessel *Imo* were in collision in Halifax Bay resulting in the *Mont Blanc* igniting then the explosion of her 5,000 tons of TNT. and ammunition. The blast decimated the entire north side of Halifax. 2,500 were killed outright together with 8,000 injured and 2,000 simply disappeared. In a school only ten survived out of the 500 children attending on that day. Across the bay on the other shore a further 200 children were killed. At a church orphanage, the matron, staff and every child perished.

Rolling stock on the railway was blown away through the air to a distance of two miles. The *Imo* was blown ashore in one piece but the *Mont Blanc* completely disintegrated as explosive forces blew her apart killing everybody on board. Many ships in the harbour were sunk; some losing their entire crew. The shock waves could be felt 100 miles from the scene. These were the shattering statistics describing the devastation of this ammunition ship blowing up. It was sufficient to make us aware that our cargo would be hazardous! Later my experiences would be extended to include the utter horror of such a scene.

"Anyone ready?" yelled the Mate. "Launch is waiting if you are going ashore." Down the ship's ladder like monkeys we climbed into the boat and soon we were speeding towards the landing stage. We couldn't wait for the ship to pull alongside when this offer was made quite unexpectedly.

Our first stop was the drug store and we ordered strawberry milk shake with apple pie and ice cream. We just couldn't believe our presence in paradise. Delights were dispensed that only dreams could realise. It wasn't mere fantasy, because each day, raisin pie and ice cream, chocolate and exotically flavoured milk shakes were savoured with a relish that only the deprived could appreciate. This was sheer ecstasy or perhaps heaven on earth had come true. Furthermore, the fruit we had begun to consider extinct, namely the banana, was actually located and devoured. At night, it was amazing to see the myriad of lights with no thoughts of blackout. It was enough just to stare at the exuberance of life without restrictions; it was so spectacular that further thoughts of entertainment didn't arise. This was an incredible world and so startlingly different from home where we were paralysed by war, its economies, rationing and blackout. This was such a contrast that it was difficult to assimilate. The wonder of it all begged the question " Did we ever enjoy this standard of living back home?" Certainly, I couldn't remember the luxuries of Drug Store cuisine. The lighting and neon signs at one time may have been present but it seemed so long ago that those memories had dimmed and faded.

As loading had started, reality soon asserted itself. The cargo was bombs, Amotol, explosives, TNT. ammunition, grenades and packaged weapons. Derricks worked night and day swinging the crates aboard. Down the holds everything was fitted and packed tightly to avoid movement. It took several non- stop twenty -four hour days to complete the work. Lower and lower sank the old ship "Nordlys" until it was fully laden. It was time to batten down the hatches with everything secured. Then, much to my surprise, enormous threatening tanks with their heavy caterpillar tracks, were being squeezed on deck. They were made fast by wire hawsers which were coupled to fittings welded on to the metal deck, not just on the forward decks but throughout the entire length of the ship, wherever space could be found. The final loading included aircraft. Dropped on top of the hatches, they were then lashed down and fastened securely to withstand the battering seas. I looked at the diminished freeboard and gasped at how deeply we had sunk to accommodate this tremendous load. My eyes searched along the outside of the ship's hull for the Plimsoll line. It was only just visible, but well below the surface of the water. This seemed to contravene Winter North Atlantic seaworthiness and shipping safety. Naively, I asked the Mate why the Plimsoll line was so far under water. He replied tersely. "That is the least of our worries. We have the Atlantic to cross. Have you seen our cargo? **This is War!"**

ATLANTIC BATTLE

The steady throb of our engines in the middle of the night confirmed that we were under way and stealthily putting out to sea. Dark sinister shapes furtively appeared then faded out of sight into the blackness. Manoeuvring his ship into position was one of the hazards that a Captain had to endure. Collision with the ship ahead, astern or on either side was a constant threat. Skilfully our position in the convoy was achieved but a sigh of relief was the only reward.

Ahead lay the North Atlantic. 3,000 miles of ferocious seas and atrocious weather. These were the risks which sailors have always accepted, but in these merciless times we had the expectations that several ships in this convoy would be sunk through enemy action. How many of us would survive this crossing? Although actual statistics at the time were not known or discussed, it would not have surprised any of us had we discovered that in the previous month our losses had averaged five Merchant Ships sunk each day.

I looked into the distance seeing ships spread out ahead. The formation of twenty-six Merchant ships was five columns wide and each column was five ships long. We were the fifth ship in the starboard column. This rear outside position was known ominously as `coffin corner' this was because attacking submarines found ships in this remote outside position an easier target. Less timid U.Boat commanders on the other hand, would surface within the convoy at night and move up and down the columns to choose the most prized victim. Asdic, the device for detecting submarines under water, was invalid in these circumstances. At night the shape of a conning tower or a slender periscope was virtually invisible in these dark waters. Thus even keeping a sharp lookout did not readily locate stalking U.Boats until the advent of short wave radar.

Ours was a slow convoy proceeding at only five knots which is simply a good walking pace. This meant we could easily be overhauled by pursuing submarines capable of three times our speed. They could also outrun the corvettes and to date they had shown no fear whatsoever of them.

Distributed around the convoy, our escorts consisted of a destroyer ahead and another astern with two corvettes patrolling on each side. In view of the losses suffered by our Merchant Ships, after four years of war, it was hardly surprising that we had little faith in the Navy's ability to provide the protection we expected.

Unfortunately, the Royal Navy's reputation was also tarnished by its alleged desertion from convoy PQ.17. Ships of the Merchant Navy were left to proceed on their own. The Germans saw that the convoy was without protection and systematically set about the massacre of almost the entire convoy. Only eleven survived out of thirty-six ships. No warship was lost. Twenty-three Merchant vessels were sunk. The order to withdraw support was given by Admiralty H.Q. Apparently, it was thought that the German Pocket Battleship, Tirpitz located in Norway, might attack. In the event, it did not leave its anchorage. The R.N. Commanders involved felt the actions they were ordered to take were the hardest and most distressing of their lives even before the true situation unfolded. Other R.N. personnel felt seriously disgraced but obeyed orders.

PQ.17 was a vital heavily laden convoy and had mustered for its pprotection as distant cover, two battleships, an aircraft carrier, six cruisers, fourteen destroyers thirteen submarines and eight Catalinas. The close escort was formed by six destroyers, four corvettes, two submarines, three rescue ships, an oiler, two anti-aircraft ships, minesweepers and trawlers. Seldom if ever, could such an array of the Royal Navy, be found allocated to secure the safe passage of one convoy. It was therefore hardly surprising that the Americans, who lost some ships in the terrible destruction, were now reluctant to leave their vessels in Royal Navy custody. They also withdrew the U.S. naval forces operating on the main transatlantic route and were hostile to multinational escort groups.

Likewise, protection from the air for merchant shipping fell short of what might have been expected. Those in command at the Admiralty and Airforce were at loggerheads, each pursuing its own agenda and failing to co-operate with each other. If aircraft carriers had been made available, then air cover for each convoy would have been possible. Also `Bomber' Harris was hell-bent on arranging 1000 bomber raids as the means to defeat Germany. He resisted the release of any Lancaster VLR bombers {very long range) to protect convoys.

American Liberator VLR aircraft, were not available but were being deployed in the Pacific. In retrospect, it was proved that for each long range bomber affording convoy cover, six merchant ships could have been saved. The value of lives and the gigantic costs per ship and cargoes far outweighed any possible destruction by bombing. What difference would 950 bombers make instead of 1000. It is horrifying that the omission of our air cover was permitted. The presence of one aircraft would keep the U.Boats submerged and could render them impotent.

Sadly, the German bombing of merchant ships was all too effective, since their Kondor aircraft could circle 2000 miles of ocean sinking merchant ships and reporting convoys to the submarines. Closer inshore, Focke Wulfs exacted their score in dive- bombing raids and German aircraft dropped Magnetic mines around our shores for good measure.

FACING DEFEAT March 1943.

The months of March, April and May, 1943, were the most critical for the Battle of the Atlantic and consequently, the final outcome of the war. This was the period of the greatest and most crucial convoy battles. In the first ten days of March 1943, forty-one ships were sunk. In the following ten days fifty-four ships were sunk. A shattering ninety-five ships or over half a million tons lost in the North Atlantic in the first twenty days of the month. The losses of merchant ships overall in March 1943 reached 129.

At the height of the Battle of the Atlantic, we reached our lowest ebb. The German submarines in March '43 were numerous enough to overwhelm our escorts. Generally, it was understood that escorts had to outnumber U.Boats by two to one. There is little wonder that in the first year of the war MN. losses averaged one ship per day, in the second year two ships per day and in the third year three ships per day. In fact in 1942 we were losing ships faster than we could replace them. This was our route to disaster. Ominous clouds of disaster gathered around us in March 1943 as shipping losses mounted. Donitz brought to bear the largest Wulf Packs yet encountered and wrought a devastation which tolled our bell of doom.

The largest convoy battle and greatest action took place involving convoys SC 122 and HX 229 consisting of ninety merchant ships and sixteen escort vessels. They were confronted by the powerful onslaught of thirty-eight German submarines which moved in to the attack. The timing was mid March 1943 These two convoys were unfortunately, close together, possibly only seventy miles apart. `SC' was a slow convoy separated a few hours sailing from the fast `HX' convoy. The vast area of sea which the ships occupied offered a larger than usual target for the lurking U.Boats. An unremitting onslaught began and continued until **twenty-two** ships had been sunk. There was no effective retaliation. Also, one escort was lost and a trawler was overcome by the weather. The jubilant U.Boat crew's confidence mounted. This was a great tactical triumph and an impressive victory for the Wulf packs. It appeared that the number of submarines at large in the Atlantic could now bring this one sided battle to its final conclusion.

The naval escorts had been able neither to protect the merchant ships nor to destroy any of the attackers. The submarines pressed home their attacks and eventually left unscathed, apart from one which was sighted by a Liberator aircraft from Iceland and sunk. Losing so many ships despite extra protection, especially arranged for these convoys, certainly shook the Admiralty's confidence. Staff believed therefore, that the credibility had gone out of the convoy system as an effective form of defence. This was in essence, tantamount to an admission of defeat. Our guardian forces in the Battle of the Atlantic were teetering on the brink of defeat!

We merchant seamen were not fully cognizant with these facts but there were distinct feelings of unease, germinated by a background of events and personal experiences that fuelled our suspicions. We felt that we had earned and were due greater respect and protection. After all we did fetch half of the food, necessary, if Great Britain was to be fed. Likewise we transported across the Atlantic the bombs and the materiels of war. Furthermore, before any aircraft could fly, a tank move or vehicle function, then fuel was necessary. Only the merchant ships made these things possible. The U.K. at that time, had no other source of oil.

Rudyard Kipling fully understood that the vital function of the Royal Navy was to protect the Merchant Ships:

Big Steamers....
Then what can I do for you, all you Big Steamers
Oh, what can I do for your comfort and good?
Send out your big warships to watch your big waters
That no one may stop us bringing you food.

For the bread that you eat and the biscuits you nibble
The sweets that you suck and the joints that you carve
They are brought to you daily by all us Big Steamers
And if anyone hinders our coming you'll starve...

-oOo-

THE AIRGAP OR DAS TODESLOCH. (The Death Hole).
Every convoy at this time was suffering attack after attack by larger groups of submarines. Admiral Donitz now had 400 submarines available, instead of only twenty-three operational at the outset of war. He was also launching twenty new submarines every month. His sole purpose was to sever our transatlantic artery, thus starving us of food and materiels of war.

Our particular convoy was just entering the Airgap south of Greenland. This was the area devoid of air cover and that was where the submarines were sinking the majority of their victims. We did not know the vast numbers, nor disposition of submarines strewn across these vicious waters. We knew of the dangers but this was the job to be done and we had volunteered to do it, so determined to defeat the U.Boats, we would doggedly fight our way across.

Thus, as each day passed, we were venturing further into the Atlantic and entering the most dangerous area. The constant awareness of the menace lurking beneath these merciless waters, screwed our nerves up to the tension of full alert. Despite this sense of readiness there was our willingness to accept what seemed to be the inevitable.

There were of course diversions such as the signalling and flag hoists. These were run up by the Commodore's ship. This was positioned central in the front row. Immediately the signal hoist appeared, it was a matter of personal pride to identify the flags, read the message and haul up our copy. Satisfaction was achieved when we responded faster than those ships around us.

The daylight hours provided these welcome distractions whereas the nights seemed more ominous. During darkness, even when fast asleep, any change of engine speed meant a distinct alteration to that steady throbbing pulse of the ship. Immediately, one was wide awake, listening for an explanation. The realisation soon dawned that more revolutions had been called for to catch up with the ship ahead or to ease off, if drawing too near.

Whoomph! whoomph! Depth charges blew up one after the other. It was obvious that we were under attack. Then the whole ship seemed to leap out of the water and vibrate in every plate. Down below, one was deafened by what sounded like a great sledgehammer being hurled against the metal of the hull.

Whoomph! whoomph! Those were so near that presumably, a

submarine had penetrated the convoy. On and on throughout the night the sounds of battle continued until daybreak. Not surprisingly, everyone slept fully clothed, complete with life jacket, clip on light and whistle. The cabin door was held ajar with a stout brass hook, in the hope that an explosion would not leave it jammed shut. A small ditty bag containing Discharge Book, Identity Papers, chocolate and cigarettes, was on hand ready for the quick exit.

Suddenly, there was a *terrific* thump with an even greater **whoomph!!** The resulting vibrations rattled through the entire ship as it shook and resonated for what seemed several minutes. Some poor devil had got the hammer! Dashing up on deck to check that we were unharmed, it was obvious that the victim was the ship alongside us, in the adjacent row. She was on fire and sinking. Still the convoy moved on whilst a corvette pursued the quarry. Depth charges were being launched right and left as it dashed across our rear. The explosions from these were rather too close for comfort but better gaping plates than gaping holes! It seemed obvious as the battle progressed, that a strong group of submarines was involved. Counter-attacks were under way in every direction. The destroyers and corvettes, hunting and depth-charging, pursued the stalkers with a vengeance that kept the escorts fully engaged. We also hoped that it would persuade the submarine commanders to keep their heads down and periscopes below.

Whoomph! whoomph! The battle sounds accompanied our daily routine work. Ashore, it might be likened to a bombing raid. The difference was, it continued all day and night after night. There was no respite and even overlooking the hazardous cargo, these wintery waters took no prisoners. All the time we were aware, that if it was our turn, there would be no tomorrow. Large ships had, perhaps, more chance of survival. A torpedo in a small 4,000 ton or lesser sized vessel, results in a quick sinking and would leave little of the the ship remaining afloat, but of course there was no point in weighing our survival chances. Survival wasn't an option. One would have to escape the initial blast of the torpedo and then somehow evade those hungry combers with sub zero temperatures. The seas at the moment were mountainous. Those slim hopes, on reflection, were dashed as one thought about our cargo, which surely had the final answer.

Whoomph!, that was another tremendous explosion! This time it was the next but one ahead of us. No.2 ship in our column. It blew up as the torpedo struck. A gigantic upheaval of sea and debris erupted and soared aloft into the heavens. Within seconds, there followed another frightening explosion, possibly a second torpedo or perhaps the boilers of the stricken ship exploding. The sea itself was transformed into a seismic wave, spreading outwards in all directions with devastating fury. As we witnessed the awful destruction, our thoughts were with the doomed seamen who had been sacrificed. Our sorrow also extended to that fine vessel now sadly in its dying agony.
The stern of the sinking ship was already under water and the bow was rising slowly vertically, as she slipped under the ocean. Carefully we approached her, hoping that there would be signs of life either in the sea or on what remained of her superstructure. The Atlantic was swallowing her hull almost in one gulp.

Nothing, just nothing! Not even a movement from bodies floating in the water. One, closely examined, was rigid in the icy waters which was hardly surprising, since the cold of the North Atlantic claims victims within minutes.

Flotsam and debris was scattered all around but we saw no sign of those we might possibly have rescued. Always there is doubt as to whether or not to stop. Ultimately, this is the decision of the captain. Advice in the circumstances has shown that any vessel stopping to pick up survivors is almost invariably torpedoed itself. The increased risk of stopping and presenting yourself as the next target makes choice difficult especially where help could be offered. The decision on this occasion was obvious. Careful observations showed no one could be retrieved, so we speeded ahead to regain our station in the convoy.

Already, ten per cent of our ships had been sunk and the U.Boats had just started their attacks. The next few days or even the next two weeks did not look at all favourable. Memories of previous battles filled us with foreboding making us realise that we would have to be very fortunate if we were going to survive. Luck does not hold out indefinitely and each time an Atlantic crossing was made, the odds were shortened.

The present encounter continued throughout the following days. Each successive attack became more threatening. Anticipating the inevitable we hung on waiting to suffer that sudden ear bursting explosion and hot searing blast which would blow us upwards to disintegrate in a fiendish cloud of extinction. Each day and each night that followed, heightened expectations. Our time was running out, yet, again and again the attacks came but somehow the U.Boats seemed to be thwarted from claiming another hit.

We steamed ahead, grateful for the respite of two days' relative peace but haunted by thoughts of those less fortunate. Somewhere, someone would be hanging on to flotsam, alone in the ocean, agonizingly cold and drowning slowly with no hope of being picked up. On rafts or ships' lifeboats torpedoed seamen perished more often than they were rescued. Having risked their lives in perilous seas and atrocious weather these dangers were now heightened by the merciless U.Boat sinkings. Torpedoing a ship could mean around fifty crew dangerously close to extinction. Cargoes could be replaced, but the expense eventually has to be paid by austerity and belt pinching somewhere.

Ships were becoming scarce. To date, they were being sunk faster than they could be replaced. The real disaster, however, was lives and human sacrifice. The sailors were a breed apart, courageous men, fighting against terrible odds in their cumbersome slow moving ships. Yet without their seamanship, skills and self sacrifice, Britain would not survive.

The Admiralty was so concerned that a directive to Captains of all Merchant ships, emphasised the need to ensure the escape of Radio Officers at the last stage of abandoning ship. Sparks were being lost through their sense of duty, transmitting SOS calls when the last chance to escape had closed. Trained men were irreplaceable. Overall this was true. It could apply equally to engine room staff who could be trapped in the bowels of the ship. Warnings applied wherever lives could be saved. Personnel numbers, above all else, crashed below sustainable limits. One third of all Merchant Seamen would ultimately perish in this service. Although still regarded as civilians, the Merchant Navy became known as the Fourth Service, suffering the highest percentage casualties of all. In fact, lives lost at sea exceeded those previously lost in sea battles over the last 500 years.

On big ships, apart from the merchant seamen, passengers or troops were carried. The largest loss of passengers and troops was from the "Lancastria" when 2,833 were drowned, or the "Laconia" with 2,276 lost. These statistics do not include the 32,000 Merchant Seamen who lost their lives during the war.

HINDSIGHT.
Only now in retrospect, by reading historical notes, can we find some explanations for the course of our battle. It transpires that at least eleven U.Boats persisted in the attack of our convoy, but being detected and pursued, they were driven off. Donitz concluded that to have hunted and attacked so many U.Boats with such astonishing certainty, some new form of detection must have been developed, since this had never happened before. Usually, only a Flower class corvette approached the submarine and the U.Boats with their superior speed had little to fear and treated them with contempt. These corvettes were an adaptation of a 925 ton whale

catcher. They rolled excessively and were designed for coastal work but they were forced into ocean escort operations. When serving in the North Atlantic, particularly in winter, conditions on board would be very uncomfortable and hardly conducive to concentration.

The Admiralty also eventually suggested that Historians would be likely to single out April and May 1943 as the critical period when we were able to fend off U.Boat attacks for the first time. Escorts with HF/DF (high frequency direction finding) could now listen to the radio transmissions of the U.Boats and trace their positions. Thus a degree of timidity and respect for our escorts was being imposed. We were unaware of these changing circumstances and in the absence of information we were not relieved of anxiety. The early losses of the ships in our convoy seemed ominous. The strength of these encounters from every direction and the number of times that we were under pressure highlighted our vulnerability, particularly, since many more days running the gauntlet remained before our destination could be reached. Clearly, many more U.Boats were now operational in the North Atlantic. Further skirmishes kept us on our mettle throughout the passage.

In the months ahead, several further battles followed before the realisation filtered through that our defences were gaining the upper hand. Losses didn't disappear; they merely diminished from the peak in March '43 to an average loss of one ship per day. As our losses decreased, the number of submarines destroyed increased. Naturally it was not long before they reacted, bringing a few innovative surprises which meant further threats to our shipping and these new threats had to be countered.

Benefiting from hindsight, we can unravel the various pressures which influenced reactions. Why were the escorts apparently more successful in fending off the U.Boats? Why were we battling through the Atlantic encountering heavier and more frequent attacks which were not pressed home with sinkings? After all,

U.Boat numbers were at their peak in the North Atlantic in the spring of 1943.

Losses of ships within the convoy were usually clearly visible. Submarine sinkings on the otherhand were not so readily observed. The escort's triumphs in our present encounter yielded a successful retaliatory kill of three submarines. We did not see all the kills. Some might have occurred on the approaches or the far side of the convoy and we did not witness these successes. Of course, until now, U.Boat victims were not expected. The escorts however, by thwarting the attackers, at least averted further sinkings and this created the scent of victory in our nostrils. Conversely, the German submarines unaccustomed to losses in their Wulf Packs were finding that they were no longer hidden or immune. They became the hunted and not the hunters.

VICTORY IN SIGHT

It started with Admiral Donitz mustering the FINK Group of forty-four submarines together in the North Atlantic. *This was the largest pack of U.Boats* ever assembled to attack a convoy. Other packs also became involved particularly with the convoy which was ONS5. Forty ageing tramp steamers were en route to Canada/USA. The convoy was first sighted 29th April 1943, some 500 miles East of Cape Farewell which is at the Southern tip of Greenland. The Wulf Pack lay in wait just East of Newfoundland.

When the U.Boats radioed to one another and back to Donitz HQ. our decoders at Bletchley Heath could now decipher their calls. The 3rd Support Group of five Destroyers was sent out from Newfoundland to assist ONS5. Subsequently on the 4th May the 1st Support Group was also sent out to assist. This was a sloop, a cutter and three frigates. They arrived on 6th May.

One of the greatest battles followed and was fought under dreadful conditions, with the weather ranging from storms to fog. Initially, the U.Boats felt that because of their numbers and likely superiority the escorts would be overwhelmed. The sinkings started and twelve Merchant ships were sunk. From the perspective of the submarines, the early losses inflicted, fuelled their confidence. Thus they believed that they could scupper the remainder of the convoy on the following day.

The next day fog had descended and the U.Boats could not locate the convoy. Visibility left them at a disadvantage because the escorts, fitted with the latest radar and HF/DF, could find the Submarines. Huff/Duff was the newly developed oscilloscope direction finding apparatus and together with centimetric radar, we had technological superiority. We could find the U.Boats despite the fog.

The final outcome of this battle found the submarines licking their wounds having suffered seven losses. Previously, on such occasions they had escaped unscathed. Thus, the escorts for the first time established that counter strikes and retaliatory sinkings could be achieved. Escorts were no longer a push over and the "happy times" for U.Boats were finished.

The final score was twelve merchant ships lost but in reply six U.Boats were destroyed and this was a new experience. Additionally, one submarine had been sunk by Coastal Command in the early passage of the convoy. Furthermore, two submarines collided in their massed onslaught thus providing bonus kills. Altogether, nine submarines were despatched and this constituted our first victory. It is doubtful whether individual U.Boat commanders realised how successfully they had been punished. On both sides it required time for losses and casualty numbers to filter through and be evaluated.

Consequently, as they were unable to continue with ONS5, immediately, the packs moved South to attack SC129, which was our convoy. The Germans had always been able to decipher Admiralty radio links and throughout the war knew the number of ships in our convoys, number and strength of escorts and date of departure of our convoys. Strangely, the Admiralty was unaware that it was itself passing on this information to the enemy.

With hindsight, we learn that the enemy on this occasion, benefitted from knowing that we were under way and our whereabouts. An explanation of the battle with our convoy SC129 also emerges. At least eleven U.Boats got through and the first two kills whetted their appetite. Again and again they launched attacks and with their superior numbers more sinkings seemed inevitable. What they did not bargain for was the loss of three of their submarines and of our reinforced counter attacks which were changing the history of the Battle of the Atlantic. Despite many attempts, they found themselves being driven off by the escorts. This was primarily because of improved technology which enabled the location and destruction of the attackers and also because of the escort's better tactical organisation. Altogether these factors increased the escorts' confidence. This included updated radar, HF/DF and the latest system of depth charging.

The U.Boats, having lost three of their pack in our convoy battle, acquired a degree of timidity and respect for their enemies. They were surprised to be so readily located and then boldly harassed with threats and kills. Thus, despite increased numbers of U.Boats and opportune targets sighted, more attacks did not yield more sinkings.

When we were under attack, Aircraft Carrier H.M.S."Biter" left a fast nearby convoy to render assistance. She was with our convoy from two o'clock in the afternoon of the fourteenth of May until eleven thirty on the morning of the sixteenth of May,1943. The carrier's aircraft were of great value in routing the enemy. When aircraft appear the U.Boats disappear.

Escort and Senior Officer's ship H.M.S. Hesperus B2 Group.
U.Boats sunk U.186 by H.M.S.Hesperus. 12/5/43.
" " " U.266 by Liberator of 86 squadron R.A.F. 14/5/43.

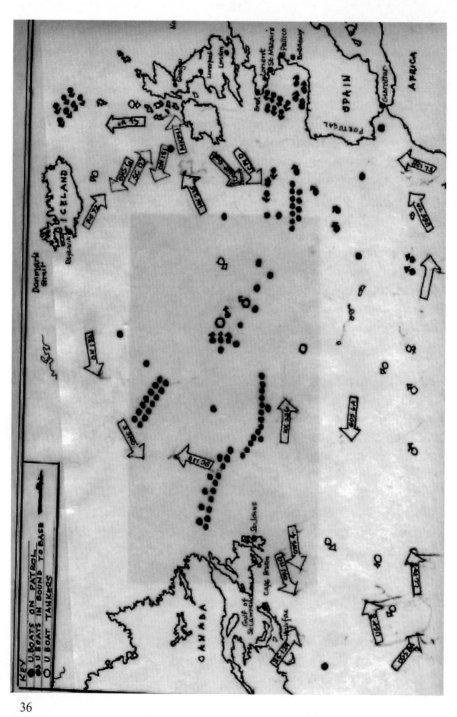

DIAGRAM SHOWS ACTION STATIONS AT 0800, ON MAY 1ST,1943 ON THE ATLANTIC.

118 U-Boats were in the Atlantic on 1st May.

Convoy ONS 5 comprising 42 merchant ships and twelve warships, lost thirteen merchant ships but the escorts and supporting forces sank seven U-Boats.

This was the prelude to a running battle during the weeks of May when convoys SC 128 and my own convoy SC129 were repeatedly attacked. We left Halifax on 2nd of May and arrived home at the end of that month.

Final outcome was that Allied forces gained the advantage so that submarine losses convinced Donitz that he should withdraw his U-Boats from the Atlantic. This was a temporary arrangement when his stranglehold was broken but they were to return later.

SUCCESS CONFIRMED

SC130 was an East bound convoy about ten days astern of ourselves and consisting of forty-five ships. They were able to fight through without any loss. Commander Gretton, leading B7 escort group, which successfully defended ONS5, was again involved. On this occasion they destroyed two U.Boats. A further three U.Boats were sunk by escorting aircraft. Donitz's twenty year old son was in one of these submarines which was lost with all hands.

During the month of May 1943, fifty Merchant ships were lost and forty U.Boats destroyed. This was an unacceptable loss of submarines and exceeded their replacement rate. Thus, the end of May 1943 is remembered as the victorious stage of the Battle of the Atlantic.

The Admiralty eventually suggested that April and May 1943 would be regarded as the critical period when we were able to fend off U.Boat attacks for the first time. Donitz realised that his U.Boats were being detected promptly and with an astonishing certainty. Hitherto this had been unknown. He guessed that the British now had a new efficient locating device. It was these sentiments which had him switch submarine strategy, primarily though only temporarily, to other waters.

Several further battles ensued in the months and years ahead and losses continued. They declined from the peak in March 1943, to an annual daily average of one per day until the end of the war. Even three days after the Germans surrendered, three merchant ships, were sunk on the 7th May 1945.

HIGH FREQUENCY DIRECTION FINDING.(HF/DF).

More escorts were now being equipped with HF/DF. Unknown to the Germans, we could now listen to the radio transmissions of the U.Boats and trace their positions. We were also able to decipher enemy transmissions so that convoys could be diverted.

THE HEDGEHOG

The Hedgehog multi-mortar system could throw depth charges ahead from the escort vessel to fall and encircle the target. Twenty-four canisters could be fired 250 yards ahead, thus avoiding the need for the escort having to pass right over the submerged U.Boat whilst trying to maintain contact up to the point of firing.

Improved depth charges which could be set to 500 ft so that U.Boats could not dive beyond danger became available.

AIR COVER

The Airgap was at last closing, since Aircraft (VLR) in the form of Liberators and Lancasters were enlisted for our protection. Aircraft Carriers sailing with important convoys menaced and destroyed submarines with their planes. Aircraft fitted with centimetric radar were especially effective over the Bay of Biscay resulting in numerous kills. The U.Boats leaving and returning to base were swooped upon unexpectedly and bombed, creating panic and inflicting losses. Eventually, it was reckoned that the submarines had only a one in six chance of returning to base.

Improved tactics and organisation of the escorts made the U.Boats respect our guardians. Aircraft newly arrived on the scene proved their effectiveness. **A VLR. Aircraft, escorting convoys in the middle of the Atlantic in its service lifetime could save six merchant ships.** Overall, aircraft sank many more submarines than our escorts. **This was a lesson that Whitehall was too late in learning.**

CONVOY contnd.

Our convoy SC 129 steamed onwards, having struggled through the Air Gap or "Das Todesloch" (The Death Hole) which was the name U.Boat commanders had for the area. The greatest concentration of submarines was in that location whilst fifty per cent were distributed over the remainder of the wide Atlantic. Several days more remained in which the worst could be expected. Awaiting us, more wulf packs were between us and our final destination.

Ahead, a signal is seen. Binoculars are focussed on the Commodore's ship as he runs a flag hoist aloft. Our response is rapidly hauled up and beaming smiles of satisfaction spread around our bridge. Quickly, the code book is scanned and interpretation is found. "The convoy is making too much smoke." The watchword is "Vigilance," if we are going to win through. There is no excuse for careless enthusiasm. No doubt the change of watches meant fresh stokers arriving in the stokehold and piling on coal at the start of their duty. Even when a ship is out of sight below the horizon, her rising telltale column of smoke can be seen. This is a dead give-away for a convoy.

But something is wrong! We are swerving sharply to starboard. A loud blast on the ship's siren confirms this manoeuvre. Now, we are hoisting two black balls, one above the other up the stay. We are out of control! Engines suddenly stop. Gradually the ship slows down and we are coasting to a halt. Stationary and wallowing in the Atlantic swell, we can now only watch as the convoy continues and is soon receding into the distance. We are being left, isolated in this vast void of ocean. Alone and fearful, the feeling of nakedness mounts. We are surrounded only by the sea and there is nothing to interrupt this helpless isolation. We heave and roll ominously in the threatening Atlantic swell. Stragglers don't survive! Put such thoughts out of mind.

The destroyer astern of the convoy approaches and is just visible on the horizon. He is signalling, his light flashing towards our ship. I dashed into the chart room and grabbed the Aldis lamp. In reply to his question, I sent in Morse the message "Steering fault." He acknowledged and sent "Be quick!" " Good luck!" I flashed an acknowledgement and tks. We would need all the good luck in our despair in the presence of unseen danger.

The 1st Mate was scampering down from the bridge and dashing along the deck. The bo'sun followed and coming up from the engine room, the Chief and Second engineer, tools in hand, ran aft towards the steering quadrant. We have the ancient rod and chain operated steering gear. Its sloppy joints are just about able to cope. A coupling has come apart and will have to be replaced. There is nothing like seeing your convoy disappearing into the distance to effect a speedy repair. The strained looks of anxiety on the faces of the engineers reveal all. They are under terrible pressures with the survival of the ship and its entire crew in their hands. This happened on the trip outward bound for Halifax and thanks to their speed and skill we did catch up with the convoy.

Faces can be seen looking over the ship`s side, peering into the dark sinister seas, hoping a tin fish won't appear. If spotted now, we are a stationary, defenceless target. Any U.Boat can approach to within optimum firing distance then taking time and with careful aim, claim a victim with a catastrophic explosion which would confirm their achievement.

The minutes race by as we keep hoping to restart. We need to achieve this quickly, before the convoy completely disappears. It is already over the horizon with only the stern of one ship just visible. We pray that the commodore won`t alter course, or we may not find them. If wishing could speed up operations, we would not be long. But life is not that simple. Anxious minutes tick away relentlessly, until, miraculously the bridge telegraph rings "Slow ahead". What a relief, but tension remains as the convoy has still to be overtaken. Our maximum speed is seven knots which means that we will be pursuing the convoy until dusk. That is the danger time both for submarine attacks and for catching the convoy. There would be little hope of finding the convoy, if it was not located before dark.

We press on. The chief engineer coaxed every possible revolution that the old lady could muster. She vibrated and quivered along every deck with the soup and plates on the saloon table dancing with the excitement. Fortunately, there was a following sea which thrust her stern upwards and forwards, pushing limits beyond expectations. Sighs of relief settled with the blanket of nightfall as like a stray sheep rejoining the flock we were once more in the company of other ships.

Soon another disturbance brings us up sharp as depth charges belch gloom in a flurry of activity. Complacency is short lived when there is war at sea. Constant threats appear as one after the other, packs of U.Boats try to ambush our convoy. Still, we have weathered another crossing and as the main group heads for the North Passage, we turn to port for the Pentland Firth and the East coast.

It is still rather early to be congratulating ourselves, because the Netherlands and the Continental shores are too close for comfort. E.Boat Alley covers the English Channel and East coast. Fast torpedo boats appear in E.Boat Alley as if from nowhere and sink victims before any help is forthcoming. They are astonishingly quick. Surprise attacks have wrought havoc and if they do not get you, the further worry is the magnetic mine. Mines claim a surprising number of victims since they have been laid by the enemy around every major port and coast. They were still sinking ships after V.E.Day.

Magnetic mines, dropped around our coast are attracted by the powerful magnetic pull from the ship's metal hull. A ship does not need to hit the mine; it will obligingly explode as the ship approaches. The explosive force is as deadly as a torpedo with the same objective. So here we go down the East coast, hoping to avoid mines and E.Boats with our destination London.

——oOo——

2

A TANKER IS TARGET No.1 AND VOLATILE!

On my arrival home, mother asks how was it? Marvellous! just look at these silk stockings I`ve brought for you. Brother James, take a look at this Canadian leather jerkin. That should sort out any clothing coupon problems for you for years to come. The food on board was fantastic! Great bunch the `Danes' and the lads were a really friendly crew.

The door bell rings! I go to open the front door and take the telegram from the telegram boy on his red bicycle. It reads "Report 9am tomorrow morning Newcastle." Three days leave in Glasgow ends as I start to pack my washing which is barely dry.

Dad comes to the station with me and gives me a lucky thruppeny bit. He dabbles with the football coupons and his Lady Luck is probably encapsulated in that coin. Now he has parted with his luck, but this is a wager he must win. The look in his eye tells me that he is not fooled by my nonchalance. He sadly wishes me good luck and cheerio. **Even he may not know how much I will need that luck.**

The train left Glasgow Central Station and I tried to keep alert since I would have to change at Carlisle. Excitement can stimulate the adrenaline even on a railway platform. Alighting at Carlisle, I asked the porter where I could catch the next train for Newcastle. He replied that there was one just about to leave from the other platform. The porter led the dash, carrying some of my gear, whilst I struggled with the remainder.

The train was already slowly leaving the platform so we ran faster. We heaved the gear into the moving guard van. The porter was on the running board and we were already half way out of the station as he collected his tip but I felt he had earned it. The guard then let me through to the carriages where I flopped down on a seat to try to regain my breathing and composure.

I arrived at Newcastle 3.15am and staggered out of the station into the Sun Hotel. I slept until 8am breakfast. The next stop was the Newcastle Marconi office, a sober stark building with wooden bench seats. It is electrified with an air of expectation and surprise. Where will I be heading? What will the ship be like? Will my fellow Sparks be friendly?

I am waiting for the call which will be transmitted over the loud speaker system in Morse. There is always an element of fear that from the staccato of Morse symbols I might miss my name. This would be devastating as it would hint at my limitations as a Radio Officer.

"Robert Welsh!" I go into the operations room to be told that I am to board *MV.NACELLA.* She is at Wallsend which is a destination of some thirty minutes distance. I go to the shipping office to sign on articles for the voyage which will remain a secret until we are well out to sea.

I discovered that I could not sleep on board the ship as my accommodation was not quite ready. A small hotel was enlisted as the temporary alternative for a night. Meantime, this was an opportunity to seek out cousin Peggy. She dances through life, tripping the light fantastic and should be rehearsing at a local dance studio. "Do step inside. As you can see, Peggy is on the floor and they are choreographing next week's show. Should be finished in half an hour, if you don't mind waiting.". I certainly didn't mind waiting,

MV.NACELLA tanker in wartime grey and No.1 Target.

particularly since scantily clad girls bent their torsos and curves into such interesting positions. This was rather better and more enjoyable than an actual theatrical production.

"All right, girls, it will be same time tomorrow." Whereupon everyone moved to the sides of the dance floor, stripped off completely and then proceeded to get dressed. I could not believe my eyes or good fortune. I could scarcely watch for embarrassment, but I did try! Besides, sailors are men of the world, though somehow I did not feel fully fledged. This was a novelty which I would not have missed. I would no doubt describe this scene to an attentive, sex starved audience, somewhere, sometime out at sea.

Next day I was anxious to go aboard *mv.Nacella.* She was built at Wallsend by Swan Hunter for the Anglo Saxon Petroleum Company and completed on 6th of June,1943. She was a beautiful new ship and obviously was in pristine condition.8196 Grt. 465'x 59'. The accommodation was superb when compared to my last ship. The *ss. Nordlys* was a fine ship but an ancient steamer and half the size. This was a motor vessel and she would be on her Maiden voyage. That was the good news. But there was one snag. She was an oil tanker, a volatile vessel! Astute seafarers check out the river to see if a tanker is waiting to sail. Then they avoid the shipping office on that day, so that they are not enlisted.

Anyone, who has witnessed a torpedoed tanker, the horrifying explosion, a total inferno with flames 1000ft high and all the surrounding sea ablaze, would understand. Escape is unlikely, but terrifying burning is inescapable. It is the number one target in every convoy. *Nacella* was a new ship, therefore she was likely to load with aviation spirit which was *highly* volatile.

We are thus the equivalent of an ammunition ship but without the camouflage. Every tanker has a distinctive shape with the funnel and most of the accommodation housed towards the stern. The obvious design is to avoid fire by having combustible gases or sparks right aft, beyond the oil tanks. Any submarine commander can spot a tanker silhouette and he will gloat at the thought of such a prize. We will be No.1 on his hit list!

PIER HEAD JUMP

There was a slight hiccup as we moved out to anchor in the Tyne. We were awaiting the final crew members to join the ship. They would be subjected to the "Pier Head Jump." This is the modern equivalent of being "Pressed." The "Press Gang" in these circumstances was composed of the officials in the shipping office. They sometimes had virtually to shanghai crew in order to complete the complement of seamen required on board an unpopular ship. Tankers did not have many volunteers! It followed that the Shipping Office would cajole and baffle the final crewmen into boarding the Pilot launch and then take them out to join the ship. It would then be too late to turn back and at the sight of the *Nacella* they would realise that they were victims of the "Pier Head Jump."

Midship, under the bridge, was the officers' saloon. In the centre was an illuminated glass display cabinet containing a shell resting on purple baize. The caption on a brass plate read "Nacella one of the Patella group." (Genus Patellacea). Thus I became acquainted with the fact that Nacella was a shellfish and that all shell tankers were named after shells.

The origin of shell tankers and the prototype of modern tanker design dates from 1892 when the "Murex" was launched. Marcus Samuel, a London East End business man, made Victorian type jewel boxes which were studded with rare shells. He had business connections in the far East and whilst out there he saw the USA. Standard Oil Company shipping oil in forty-five gallon drums to voyage around the Cape. He realised that if he could ship oil via the Suez Canal and in bulk he could undercut that trade.

He had a ship specially designed which he showed to the Egyptian authorities. He convinced them that if it grounded in the canal there would be no blockage. Simply pump out the water ballast tanks and the ship would be refloated and the problem would be solved. Likewise, escaping oil would be trapped in cofferdams between the tanks so that pollution would be avoided. Agreement was reached. He arranged to have built a series of tankers to carry oil in bulk. These were the forerunners of modern tanker design.

He named the first ship "Murex" after a shellfish which yielded a rare purple dye used only by Royalty and much prized by Eastern dwellers. The captain was given a Murex shell which was exhibited in the saloon of the ship. This practice of naming and carrying the appropriate shell is a seafaring tradition which has evolved over the years. The shell insignia is now of course ubiquitous and can be found everywhere ashore as well as at sea.

Joining a Ship on Tyneside I soon appreciated the Geordies. Like their counterparts on the Mersey or Clyde they were genuine and had their own brand of humour and distinctive dialect which I readily understood. We certainly have diversity of peoples in the U.K. On board ship this adds spice to relationships, peppered perhaps with humorous raillery.

Wartime security means that the Blue Peter flag is not hoisted to announce sailing. Leaving, we just fold our tents like Arabs and as silently steal away. Loch Ewe was again the launch site for ships like us seeking convoys for westerly migration.

Fine summer weather meant a comfortable crossing, if one overlooks the wartime situation. On this trip, I was appointed librarian, an interesting sideline, which took up my leisure time and the reward was the pleasure it generated.

NEW YORK
The rumour circulating was "New York" and like most nautical rumours it turned out to be true. Thus our entry to the Big Apple was via the Hudson River. I was absolutely astounded and disgusted at the latex rubber surface which we encountered. The ship

ploughed through a solid mass of condoms some fifty yards wide and going on for miles. These articles being a taboo subject, made it all the more surprising. In those days, pollution was not an issue, but anyone could recognise here was a disgraceful problem.

Then, I lifted up mine eyes to behold the aesthetic skyline. The Statue of Liberty on Bedloe's Island in the middle of New York Bay, declared this to be a Freedom loving country. The Manhattan skyline, with its tallest buildings in the world, proclaimed an atmosphere of achievement. Skyscrapers, like the Empire State building, the Chrysler building with its formidable pinnacle, Rockefeller Centre and others form silhouettes which are recognised the world over. This must be the way to approach New York, up river, having this perspective and the splendour of this view.

Oil terminals with their combustible storage tanks are sited well out of town. We berthed at Perth Amboy, Port Socony. It took hours to get down town but I was beginning to realise that I was a bona fide traveller. Every day of every year was spent on the move, either at sea or ashore. Thus as a confirmed nomad, I couldn't wait to board the bus, then the ferry to see Times Square, Broadway, the delights of Radio City, or Central Park. So Manhattan, here I come.

The novelty of travelling by bus was an opportunity to observe the Americans. Amazing, but it was the fair sex, with their flimsy summer frocks, emphasising their charms, which first captured my attention. I could linger on these attractions but I was distracted by the gum chewing. Everyone was chomping away like goldfish, even old ladies chewed. Of course, gum eventually has to be parked somewhere and it is everywhere. It can be found on the underside of every table or horizontal ledge.
Yes, the girls are gorgeous but perhaps we had competition. The males in this obviously affluent society, had their barber shampoo and cut their hair. Shaving followed, with facial treatment and

naturally, they had their nails manicured. Shoe shining was automatic, since nobody seemed to brush their shoes. If one hesitated for a moment at a station or busy halt, immediately came the offer, "Shine your shoes, Sir?"

Above all else, the friendliness and hospitality of the Americans was incredible. Servicemen were treated like heroes and this included, for a change, the Merchant Navy.

Tankers turn around within the week, so time is of the essence. Besides, that ocean out there demands we make the most of living whilst we can. Therefore, I captured those skyscrapers as if they were `Munros.' It was not difficult, of course, because Radio City building has the fastest lift in the world. Sixty floors in thirty-seven seconds, was enough to make one's ears pop. After a tour and trip to the top of this skyscraper, I received from Radio City Music Hall a free ticket to enjoy the "Rockettes." This was the world famous group of thirty-six chorus girls who must delight any guy with red blood corpuscles.

The American Theatre Wing Merchant Seamen's Club, West 43rd Street,N.Y. exemplified the all American attitude of hospitality. I received another gratis ticket to see the play "Arsenic and Old Lace." Seats were in the orchestra stalls, no less. Then we moved to the Stage Door Canteen, where we enjoyed another gratis but excellent show. As the night was still young, it was back to the Club for another round of entertainment at which one rubbed shoulders with leading film and stage personalities. I had a chat with Paul Robeson, the bass negro singing film star and collected his autograph. He was one of my heroes from visits to the cinema back home. His voice was so rich and vibrant that even as he spoke, one could actually feel those vibrations.

Still awake, it was time to check out the bit of frivolity and noise coming from the stage. I went into the theatre and enjoyed another laughter tickling encounter. This time it was the "Three Follies." These girls absolutely split my sides or was it that I was in my cups by that time? All I can say, if one considers this run ashore, one gets the drift of what it means to pack in fun and enjoyment whilst there's time. Still in my late teens, obviously, midnight is too early to bring down the curtain. Long may your big jib draw and when, as now, it is drawing well, then stick with it!

Rudyard Kipling.(Anchor Song)
...

Well, ah, fare you well; we can stay no more with you, my love-
Down, set down your liquor and your girl from off your knee;
for the wind has come to say:
"You must take me while you may,
If you'd go to Mother Carey
(Walk her down to Mother Carey!),
Oh, we're bound to Mother Carey where she feeds her chicks at
sea!"

We don't actually need fair wind or fine weather but we do need a convoy. So its off to Norfolk, Virgina to link up with our convoy. Mother Carey's Chickens are soon in our wake and they are ordinarily known as the "Storm Petrel" because of the sailors' belief that their presence forecasts rough weather. Actually, they are seldom seen from the shore unless an onshore gale brings them within sight of a headland. That of course would indicate rough weather at sea. It is fascinating to see these tiny creatures living far out on the ocean with the ability to fly lightly across the surface of the huge seas. Hence the name of little Peter as they resemble St Peter's achievement of walking on the water.

A rare sight on this passage was a lone albatross with its eight feet wing span. The king stayed with us for several days. It was the time to reflect upon the belief that skippers become albatrosses and a drowned shipmate (in a new guise) may be a seagull. These birds must therefore be treated with respect and to harm them one could expect only a catastrophe would follow.

We also saw numerous flying fishes skimming two feet above the surface and travelling for some thirty yards. Tankers, when fully laden, have seas rolling over the deck almost submarine fashion. Thus we collected a number of these flying fishes on deck and it was easy to observe their winged structure. Mammals such as dolphins are fascinating to watch and these engaging creatures took up much of our attention. Surfing on our bow wave or leaping out of the sea they thoroughly enjoyed themselves.

Gibraltar on our port bow, this meant that another Atlantic crossing had been achieved. Onwards we proceeded, destination Algiers, to discharge our aviation spirit.

YOU HAVE BEEN WARNED.

WARNING THIS IS A THEATRE OF WAR.

BY ORDER. ANYONE ATTEMPTING TO ENTER OR LEAVE THE DOCKS, EXCEPT BY THE ORDINARY ENTRANCES AND EXITS, IS LIABLE TO BE SHOT.

N.B. VERY LIABLE.

This and other directives were brought to our attention, because having just won the Desert Campaign and taken over North Africa, this coast was ripe with espionage and **enemies.**

BE CAREFUL Algiers has more listening ears than Glasgow or Liverpool. Anyone who gives you drinks and asks you questions is not doing so for fun.

CARELESS TALK and you will be charged with contravention of Espionage Laws. Penalties are **very severe.**

Apart from the above welcome, the Casbah district, which might be construed as tempting to sailors, had a few covering notes.

THE CASBAH DISTRICT is very DANGEROUS at all times.

Crews are advised to move about in at least PAIRS and beware of those likely to lead them to the CASBAH DISTRICT.

CASBAH DISTRICT

Every night there are cases of Merchant Seamen who have been stripped, wounded and robbed by Arabs. Seamen are warned for THEIR OWN SAKE that the town of Algiers, in certain districts,is very dangerous at night,particularly for those who are drunk. THE CASBAH DISTRICT is very DANGEROUS at all times. Crews are advised to move about in **PAIRS** AND BEWARE OF THOSE LIKELY TO LEAD THEM TO THE **CASBAH district.**

-oOo-

Obviously, the message of these new dangers was relevant. However, it could be pointed out that since we departed Newcastle we had been in the front line of the theatre of war, apart from a few days in New York. Algiers had a fascination, because of its Arabic origins and culture. Naturally, we explored the town and the market where I purchased a pair of wooden sailing yachts, mounted on book ends. These mementoes have survived and today they function on my desk as reminders of past pleasures.

Strange things happen, as when returning with Taffy, my fellow Sparks, we were approached by a khaki clad soldier. We were on the outskirts of Algiers, in a fairly affluent district. Large houses bordered either side of the tree lined road. We were wearing white sleeveless shirts, white shorts and sandals. A British army "Tommy" approached us saying that the house opposite was a brothel which he wanted to visit. He could not enter because of the army military policeman stopping the lads in khaki. On the other hand, with our civilian gear there was nothing to prevent us gaining access. Would we mind swopping gear so that he could have his half hour of pleasure? "No problem," said Taffy who was of similar size. Without any fuss, he swopped shorts and his shirt and I soon found myself, with a bemused khaki character, for the next half hour. Of course, I warned him of hygiene hazards and the fact that the red cap fellow could have seen them doing their swop, so that he would end up in jankers. As far as he was concerned it was just a great joke. Fortunately, sitting on a wall in the warm sunshine made waiting a pleasant relaxation.

Sure enough, at the end of half an hour, there was Tommy, our combatant, satisfied and smirking as his 'mission amour' had been sweetly accomplished. Without further ado, the clothes were exchanged. Decorum on the public highway was not even given a second thought.

Life is certainly strange. One day Taffy wandered alone along the beach. The Mediterranean, as ever, beckoned a swimmer out of the heat and into the blue. So, dropping his clothes on the beach, naturally, he went in for his swim. Modesty was never a problem with Taffy. Later, refreshed and happy, he walked up the beach to dress. Gone! vanished! All his gear had been pinched.

I happened to see a number of our crew leaning over the side of our ship, gesticulating and laughing at someone strolling along the quay. They were yelling "Got a cigarette? or, "You got a cigar?" It was Taffy, completely starkers but he had acquired a notice board "NO SMOKING." with which he covered, at times, his manhood!

EXPLOSION
Stranger still, was the afternoon when I was on *Nacella's* bridge, enjoying the sunshine and gazing across towards Algiers and its harbour. We had discharged our cargo and just finished gas freeing. This was an operation where canvas chutes were erected to divert air down into the empty holds of the ship. The gases and fumes were thus blown out, although during the process, the ship

**Market
Street
Casbah**

**Lemonade
Seller
Casbah**

was in effect a gas bomb. Because of this danger, we were moored at the gas terminal some miles away from the town and main inner harbour. We were alongside this breakwater or outer quay, at the entrance to the harbour and system of docks. I noticed a disturbance some distance away. There was considerable activity involved in towing a ship out of a dock. A black pall of smoke rising from one of her forward holds spelled trouble. I watched her being towed out across a stretch of water in the docks with her tugs straining to keep way on her, for steerage. The captain was on the bridge, a crew member up front at her bow. Ahead of these vessels was a destroyer keeping the way clear to the harbour entrance. The hazardous vessel was being towed out to sea as she was an obvious threat amongst other shipping.

I watched the struggle to negotiate the harbour entrance since it narrowed at our breakwater quay. The tugs were doing an efficient job, with the destroyer standing by ahead, to divert any possible incoming vessels. As she passed *Nacella* I could see the lone figure of the captain on his bridge peering through the smoke at our tanker no doubt with apprehension at the thought of our vulnerability. I was probably the last person to see that heroic captain alive. Also, I was lucky that I did not linger to watch the scene!

She had now just past clear of our bow and the breakwater, so I went down to my cabin. Suddenly, without warning I got my first flying lesson. *Nacella,* along her entire length, seemed to leap four feet into the air. The blast and sounds of shattering glass and crashing debris almost burst my eardrums. I flew up through the air until my head struck the deck head in the cabin. Concussion overwhelmed me as with the cabin disintegrating around me, I passed out.
I was not unconscious for long because when I came to and struggled out on to the deck, it was all still happening. Cautiously, I looked over to the burning ship which was a scene of utter devastation. Glancing in the direction of the destroyer I could see that its bow had been blown clean away, killing everyone in it. The

destroyer was now barely able to keep afloat with her large forward section missing.

The might of the explosion within the burning "Fort la Monte" had left the ship a tangled mass of twisted metal. The tugs had been blown to pieces and the destroyer blown apart, but why did we escape?. We were closer to the burning ship than the destroyer. Luckily, at that stage, we were free of volatile spirit and gases. Blast performs strange tricks. We did have the breakwater between ourselves and the explosion. This by some fluke of fortune had diverted the blast up and over the top of our ship. It also explains why 8000 tons and 500 feet. of ship could be lifted bodily skywards at least four feet out of the water. The enormous suction drew the fires from out of our furnaces, engulfing the stokehold in flames and this enveloped our stoker. One of the many victims, he suffered horrendous burns. I doubt if he survived.

The sea was solid with flotsam and dead fish. Some of the motionless fish would suddenly produce spasms of torturous wriggling. Others, badly injured, were swimming with jerky movements as they slowly succumbed to a painful death. A rescue operation for any human beings in this mass of floating debris had to be undertaken. We rowed through it in a small boat collecting human parts. One body I remember particularly, as I put a rope round his neck and towed him along behind. He was wearing a singlet and I can still vividly recollect seeing his head bobbing at the transom of our boat. It was not a pleasant afternoon.

Next day cigarette tins and fish had been washed ashore. Masses of dead fish were strewn along the beach to a width of six feet and extending for at least a mile. Thousands of cigarette tins still bobbed about in the sea amongst the dead fish and flotsam. The entire beach area and adjoining bay disclosed a scene of startling chaos and utter devastation. Nobody nearby, who saw the explosion, could describe it, as they would be among the dead. One has to go five miles distance, to Algiers, to find witnesses of the event.

Onlookers in Algiers described the start as a peaceful sunny afternoon. As they looked down towards the docks from their high vantage spot, they viewed the tightly packed merchant ships with masts erect and derricks angled up to the sky. The criss cross of cables ropes and stays, resembled an intricate working web. Then a black menacing blob appeared. As it moved within the web the threatening dark patch evolved as smoke curling upwards from one of the ships.

Out at the seaward entrance to the harbour the tumbling waves lapped against the breakwater. The tanker "Nacella" was moored peacefully alongside it. Down below the stricken ship had become the focus of frantic activity and was obviously in trouble. A pall of smoke formed a black cloud as it billowed out of its forward hold. Unable to quench the fire quickly, the ship was being manoeuvred out of the docks. Fire fighting tugs with cannon hoses were projecting streams of water into the air and on to the forward section of the ship. With one tug at her bow and one attached by rope to her stern the "Fort la Monte" was being rapidly hauled out to sea. As she approached the harbour entrance the dark smoke was thickening and developing into a threatening black cloud.

A destroyer in attendance had kept the passage out of the docks clear of other vessels and as they approached the breakwater she proceeded ahead into the bay and was standing by so that the tugs could tow the "Fort la Monte" out to sea.

Suddenly, a mighty pillar of fire and flames burst upwards at the harbour entrance and curlingng grey-black smoke at its fringes and peak , it soared five thousand feet in seconds and was still rising. Wider and higher it grew as within seconds there followed the sound of a cataclysmic rolling boom to envelop the entire universe of sky and sea, with a noise so gigantic that it felt the firmament of the world had trembled. These vibrations were accompanied by the surge of a hurricane force wind, like the breath of hell sweeping over the land and sea. Buildings in its path swayed to

59

their foundations as it tore passed ripping out panes of glass and hurling them onwards before it. Trees were uprooted or bent flat whilst metal drums and baulks of timber were propelled along in the midst of this fearsome blast. From the ship's hull a seismic wave swelled outwards across the Bay of Algiers and pushed into the harbour until its waves rocked the ships and bounced them against the harbour walls, creating panic. Those witnessing the spectacle were spellbound and gasped with amazement. Then they rushed forward and seaward to obtain a better view.

When the "Fort la Monte" blew apart she was only minutes away from being clear of the harbour and out at sea. There, she could have been abandoned in safety, but it was not to be. The skeleton crew undoubtedly were aware of the time bomb they were attempting to sail out into the Bay. These Merchant Seamen bravely undertook this risk knowing that any moment could be their last. But this was their ship and their decision with the vain hope that for the safety of neighbouring ships, the docks and even the town, the vessel could be taken out to sea and abandoned.

The crew would be aware that they were sitting on **TWENTY-FIVE TONS OF AMOTOL**. This amount had the potential to devastate the entire town of Algiers. **JUST TWELVE KILOS OF AMOTOL** is enough to blow up a 10,000 ton ship out of the water. Many other Merchant Seamen have paralleled this situation and were just lucky to survive. On this occasion the price was being exacted. Torpedoes and depth charges contain Amotol which is a mixture of TNT and Ammonium Nitrate. Ammunition ships invariably have their quota of Amotol. Not a person on the "Fort la Monte" survived. Not one body was found.

Those watching from a distance could see the pillaring explosion. At close quarters, the horror was mind-searing. The entire forepart of the ship erupted and was blasted away from the rear half of the vessel. Two thousand tons of twisting metal was wrenched outwards and upwards by the volcanic force. The whole of the foredeck was folded upwards and back over the bridge leaving the gaping holds as a tangled mess. Part of the deck struck the funnel and pushed it backward so that it was now lying horizontal.

A vast expanding balloon of flame, five hundred feet across and growing, flowered out from the ship. It swept across the destroyer scorching everyone in its path. Thirty crew members were killed in the explosion and all but two of the officers. More than eighty others were grievously injured. The blast from the stricken ship virtually blew the bows clean off the destroyer and there was little remaining. Liquid fire searched through every passage of the-destroyer and searing round every passage it poured into the mess decks. Darting tongues of flame licked through the galley and leaped over the bridge. The magazine container of Oerlikon shells was set off in a series of explosions followed by the staccato cracking from the ammunition lockers.. Shells were exploding in every direction.

The tugs were not immune to the horrendous blast. The nearest to the "Fort la Monte" completely disappeared. Her crew were never found. The other tug further out had her bridge and super-structure blown off, leaving nothing above her deck level. She now appeared like an abandoned coal barge.
Pieces of the ship now showered down from the ten thousand feet cloud of smoke which darkened the sky. A seaman hosing the decks of his ship nearly two miles away, was sliced in two by a lump of falling steel. No windows in the city remained intact. One of my colleagues was thrown through a shattered shop window in the main street. To the citizens in the street it sounded like the end of the world. Two hundred miles away, in Oran, people ran out of their houses to investigate when they heard the sound.

Lying alongside the breakwater, at the entrance to the harbour, was the *mv. Nacella* notching up yet another close call in her battle for survival.

MINES

We left Algiers and sailed along the N.African coast to Bizerta. The whole of this area had been mined by the Germans to protect their own supply ships. Mines had also recently been laid by the allies to foil the enemy and their E.Boats. We just hoped that our route had been effectively swept clear. It was no exaggeration to describe the coast as a dangerous area.

Entering **Bizerta,** wrecks seemed to be everywhere as they could be seen strewn around in the shallows. It was reckoned that there were twenty-six sunken ships to be avoided. Some had been scuttled by the Germans to put the port out of action, but it was unseen submerged hulks which were the navigators' nightmare. The obvious half-submerged ships and the utter devastation all around presented a sickening scene of destruction. Some hulks had large holes torn out of their hulls by the explosions and their wreckage was witness to almost mindless waste. Both sides had contributed to this aftermath of war, particularly in the last few months before occupation. At that stage Bizerta was practically bashed out of existence. Navigating a vessel into the inner lake through the narrow entrance was treacherous. The lake at Bizerta was large and an ideal anchorage, although respite was not forthcoming because of the air attacks and the bedlam of bombs.

Those wanting shore leave had to be ferried across the lake in the ship's lifeboat. The journey took half an hour but on a beautiful summer's day and usually void of wind this was a pleasant trip. At night, the return journey was hilarious. Those who couldn't sing, did! Those, normally shy, led the frivolity, encouraged by the consumption of Muscatel, Vino or similar cheap local plonk. Balmy evenings and the warm Mediterranean lake combined to tempt our revellers over the side. What did we do with the drunken sailors? We removed their wallets, money and identity papers from their back pockets. We could not stop them going over the side, where they held on to the rope holds round the hull. The singing and bantering of these jolly tars was worth the trouble, except when they would swop positions or drop off into the sea. A sense of humour helped. We tried to motor full speed because they could not hang on for ever and the quicker we got them back to the ship the better. But four crew being dragged through the water impeded our progress. Soaking their paper money was not a particular problem, because bartering, especially with soap, was the important currency. However, if identity papers and photograph became sodden that would create problems.

A few days later, we left for Ferryville, to load our cargo of diesel oil and then returned to anchor at Bizerta. The build up of ships in the lake began to look significant and the enemy thought so too. As the daylight faded, the nightly drone of bombers became more pronounced, until overhead, they dropped screaming destruction on to the anchored ships. We, of course retaliated, but their numbers built up each night and eventually all hell was let loose.

Sailors confronted with the choice of a woman ashore or being bombed at sea, do not form a reliable gun crew. Thus, I received a request one night to help out with the twelve-pounder gun. Accordingly, I volunteered and went along to the stern, down into the bowels of the ship and into the ammunition locker. I then commenced to heave up supplies of four inch shells, so that our anti aircraft fire had the continuous respect of those bombers.

The next day when the gunners returned, they questioned me as to my actions. Apparently, my method of setting the charges on the shells could have blown myself and others asunder. In my ignorance, I was setting a time fuse to enable the shell to burst at the desired height without impact. It was amazing, therefore, that one hadn't detonated before going aloft. If one had been dropped or knocked... Well, I was only trying to help. "Yes," they said, "the bloody bombers!"

The entire sky overhead was a pyrotechnical display of shell bursts and speeding tracer bullets. The noise from all our ships was quite terrible and the canopy of smoke and shrapnel turned the heavens into a battling hell. Then parachute flares would be launched, so that the entire night sky would be brightly illuminated. Unfortunately, the ships then appeared clearly visible to the aircraft overhead. I cannot recollect numbers of ships damaged or sunk nor could I say without some research, how many planes were shot down. As far as *Nacella* was concerned, she was riddled with holes and with deeply gouged indentations throughout the length of her hull, funnel and superstructure. These wounds were treated with red lead. Prior to being repainted with good grey paint, she looked like a bad case of measles. There was also a plate of twisted metal some ten feet long by six feet wide blasted out of a victim ship. This metal plate smashed against the side of my cabin on our bridge. The captain seemed delighted that he too had a near miss.

We were under way again, a small convoy meaning business. It was not yet dawn but across the lake the sound of anchors being weighed announced the exodus. One after the other ships carefully negotiated their way out to the Mediterranean to join the convoy. Our destination was the Tyrrhenian Sea for the invasion of Italy at Salerno, code name "Operation Avalanche."

Our role with the invasion plans was to supply diesel fuel to the various types of landing craft. As the refuelling supply ship, we took up a suitable inshore anchorage. We were part of an armada mustered together but spreading throughout a vast area of the sea. Both Merchant ships and Royal Navy vessels were either bombarding the shore or performing a maternal role by protecting stationary ships which inevitably came under aerial attack.

The vast fleet of landing craft came alongside *Nacella,* one after the other in a constant stream to be refuelled. They varied from LCI Landing Craft Infantry, LST Landing Ship Tank, LCF Landing Craft Flak for anti aircraft offshore protection. We also supplied fuel to small fuel barges and to LCT Landing Craft Tank. It was a hectic battle and with the heavy swell heaving the small craft against our ship's sides, loading was a precarious exercise.

Later there was a real battle as the enemy tried to repulse our forces ashore. Relentlessly, the German aircraft bombed and torpedoed ships. Radio controlled bombs were introduced against our ships with astonishing effect. In reply, every vessel cracked off with everything from Pom Pom,Oerlikons, four-inch or six-inch depending upon which guns were available. It was all happening and no doubt when we left it continued with unremitting violence. Certainly, several vessels were sunk and the situation ashore was extremely tense with heavy fighting at one stage. I know that we did not linger for more than a few days and when the mission was completed, with all fuel discharged, we were underway once more, destination New York.

SEVENTH PHASE OF ATLANTIC BATTLE
Compared to the activity of the spring of 1943, the Battle of the Atlantic was relatively quiet during the summer months. However, early in September 1943, we were entering the seventh phase of the Battle of the Atlantic. The Germans had launched twenty submarines with fresh crews and the latest equipment installed in their effort to regain the initiative.

GNAT.T5
One of these innovations which was introduced and threatened our Merchant Ships was the *"GNAT.T5"* acoustic torpedo. This deadly weapon could snake through a convoy to a target, attracted by the sound of the ship's propeller. The U-Boats themselves were being punished now by our aircraft and with shattering effects on the morale of their crew.

WANZE
Donitz had **"WANZE"** gear supplied to each U-Boat. This enabled them to have early warning of centimetric radar carried by our aircraft and escorts.

ANTI AIRCRAFT

As a further boost to the confidence of a U-Boats' crew **"heavy Anti Aircraft weapons"** were fitted to each submarine to enable them to fight off attacking planes. Fortified with these weapons, a group of twenty U-Boats left to take up position 840 miles East of Cape Farewell which was virtually "Das Todesloch" (the Death Hole) familiarly known as the "Airgap.".

They lined up seventeen miles apart in a group forming the "Leuthen Wulf Pack.". Two convoys were awaited and when contact was made the result of the murderous attacks was several of our ships sunk. Others were badly damaged by these new acoustic torpedoes. We were in the vicinity on the dates in question and research pending, it seems likely that we were involved in the battles.

New York weather in the Fall was pleasantly cool, so blue merchant navy uniform was the rig of the day. Presents had to be bought, because rumour was that we would be homeward bound. Remembering my promise to Father to bring him a leather jerkin, Maceys` store seemed a likely source. I explained to the shop assistant that one size larger than my own size was required, because the jerkin had to fit father. We were happy with the one selected and it was suitably wrapped up.

"Now then what about one for yourself, sir?"
"No, that is all, thank you."
"But you are out on the bridge and a leather jerkin is excellent for the rough weather at sea."
"No, it is all right, thank you."

The shop assistant was rather persuasive and insisted that the jerkin was just what I needed and in fact, **"would last a lifetime."** "Look," I said quietly, "it might last a lifetime but then that is **no use to me.** My only hope is to be able to get this one back home.". It shook the assistant to find someone aware that he had no future. **I accepted that I was dead.** Obviously, living on the

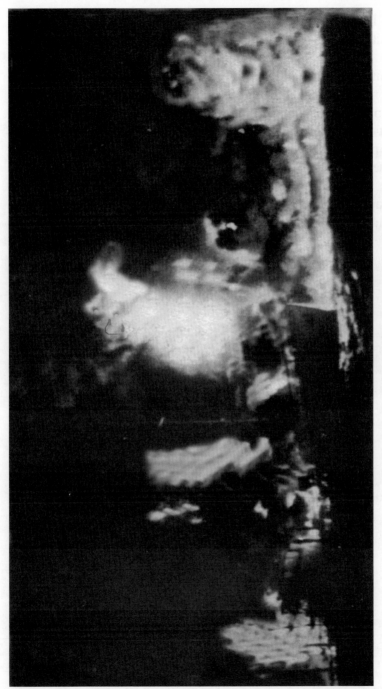

Bombed Tanker burning ferociously.

67

edge of life for many months creates an attitude of acceptance of the inevitable.

I had not realised the implications of what I had said until I saw the ashen face of the attendant at the cash register. He was whispering to his colleague and pointing towards me, indicating that he had just served a **ghost,** or at the very least someone who had **ghastly** prospects.
Well, the gods were with us once more, because another Atlantic crossing was accomplished. Arriving back home, it was a pleasure to unwrap the various souvenirs and presents which brought gasps of delight from the recipients.

3

FRIDAY SAIL, FRIDAY FAIL

Certain days are tabooed at sea. Sailors dislike starting voyages on a Friday as a variety of confused ideas involving the Flood, Crucifixion and others were said to have occurred on a Friday. Even shipping companies would not despatch passenger vessels on a Friday, any more than they would offer Cabin No.13.

I was not apprehensive when I was recalled to report at the Marconi office, Avonmouth on a Friday. After all, it was unlikely that I would be signed up and despatched on that same day. Normally, it could take several days before a voyage was organised. Thus, on arrival, I was told to find lodgings for a few days until a ship became available.

I had just settled in and I was unpacking a few items, when I heard the landlady call out, "A taxi for you, Mr Welsh!" This was a surprise and together with my gear I was quickly bundled off to Cardiff which was some sixty miles distant and on the other side of the Severn.

At Cardiff, it was sign this and sign that and back into the taxi for the docks. We stopped at the top of the quay where someone yelled, "Down here!" Sure enough, looking down the iron ladder to the dock below, I saw a chap in a motor launch with his engine running ready to take me out to the ship.

I was provided with a spray sheet to shield me from the spindrift

coming over the bow as we buffeted our way out into the sea.

Under the cover, I did not have an opportunity to sight the ship before actually bumping alongside it. Attention was then focussed on the rope ladder which was swinging down the side of the ship. This required my full concentration, if I were to escape falling into the drink. The launch was heaving up and down on the waves and it was being bashed against the ship's metal hull. I had to time my leap very carefully to be sure to catch hold of the ladder and then commence the ascent.

Reaching the top of the ladder I leapt over the bulwark and down on to the deck. Amazing, but already my gear had been hoisted up on to the ship by a rope. Struggling with my possessions, I was helped to my cabin by a chap who obviously could not speak much English. His message was "Can get food in officers' saloon, now!"

When I started to walk towards the dining saloon, the noise of a windlass, clanking away up at the bow, could be heard. The anchor was being weighed. We were getting underway. "Good life! We are setting sail on a Friday!" This shattering thought surfaced with the realization that I had been shanghaied! It was incredible how pressed and devious the operation had been, with no explanations offered. Obviously, the ship had been held up awaiting my arrival, but why?

In the saloon, I discovered that I was on an Estonian ship, the **SS.SULEV** 2000 Grt. Thus she was one quarter the size of my previous ship and a great deal older. To cap it all, it was **Friday the thirteenth**! I gleaned that my rapid appointment was because someone had declined to join the ship. The food was palatable and the officers were a cheerful collection of Estonian, Norwegian and a trio of British, including myself.

Thence I returned to take a closer look at my cabin. It had a comfortable warm feeling as I opened the door. I stepped inside and left the cool damp November air of the Irish Sea. "Where was the heater?" I pondered. Then I realised it was the funnel! This cabin had been especially constructed for wartime emergency occupation of the extra Sparks. As I lay back in bed against the side bulkhead, I was leaning against the funnel. Great, for northern climates, but what about the Mediterranean? I might find out since that was where we were heading.

My early morning cup of tea ushered in another surprise and another taboo. It was delivered and put by the side of my bunk by a woman. A woman at sea on this ship! It was enough to make the hair stand up on the back of my neck. Not to mention what it would do to the old shellbacks who would shift in Davy Jones at this latest discovery.

Woman has long been considered unlucky afloat. Skippers in the past may have been reluctant to pile on sail or take risks if there were females aboard. Having a woman on board ship was thus taboo. It is amazing, however, after gaining experience, what a sailor might do! In due course, I was able to overcome this superstition, but for the moment in time of war, this taboo looked like a definite threat. Irrespective of the fact, Scandinavians often had wives at sea, this woman was the 1st Mate's wife.

The Bay of Biscay has a reputation for rough weather but we were proceeding in spanking form. Of course, nobody dared to whistle, since "devil's music" might goad the gods into windy, dangerous retaliation. There were dangers enough because we were crossing the routes taken by the U-Boats, as they made their way out to the Atlantic from the west coast of France.

It was nice to see Gibraltar again but we dare not dwell on thoughts that these Straits were also used by submarines. Crafty U -Boat commanders utilised the currents in the Gibraltar Straits to pass in or out of the Mediterranean. They did so without the use of engines and thus eluded detection. These currents flow at four knots and are produced by differences in salinity and temperature.

Evaporation at the surface of the Mediterranean which is land-locked, results in increased salinity. The salty dense sea sinks and less salty water from the Atlantic flows in to replace both it and the loss through evaporation. Because of the less dense inflow, this cool water forms the surface current and the denser and warmer Mediterranean outflow current is at the lower level.

We did not realise that German submarine commanders were floating in and out in silence without the use of engines simply using the currents. They had perfected this ruse. Furthermore, distinct temperature differences between different depths deflects sound signals. Thus submarines can hide under a temperature change since sonar signals are deflected and foiled.

BOUGIE
Our route was along the North African coast until we reached Bougie. This was a charming little port strategically placed by nature to defend itself. It was built on a hill overlooking the harbour. Clean modern white buildings were adjacent to Arab architectural features such as domed mosques and Arab market places. Despite its peace and charm, Bougie had obviously vigorously resisted the Allied Invasion. The aftermath of fierce conflict was obvious from the wrecks and sunken ships strewn around the harbour. It was an appalling scene of waste and destruction and unfortunately this graveyard of ships is repeated in many other ports around the Mediterranean.

Ashore there were fine picturesque walks along cliff tops, where perilous drops of 100 feet down to the sea below provided an added thrill. Looking out, there was the bluest of blue seas textured in brilliant sunshine: altogether it provides me with happy memories from those lively times. Orange groves, tangerines and citrus fruits were in abundance. Figs, dates and nuts of several varieties were all succulent supplements to our normal fare. It naturally followed that the wines were exceedingly tempting so that intake exceeded control. Although mentally, faculties were

SS.SULEV, Estonian ship built 1908, 3,000 GRT. Voyage to Bougie, for iron ore.
Bomb attack my 20th Birthday, Oerlikon shells retained as souvenir

retained, I can well recollect conversing in "fluid" French with a young femme, but being quite unable to pursue her, even at walking pace. Other shipmates I have seen quite "legless" but able still to converse reasonably. Of course, extreme palatability of these wines left some who went courting ashore losing both motor control and mental ability prompting the witty comment "there rests another stoned date."

Entertainment, other than alcoholic, was enjoyed at a splendid theatre, where ENSA. performed brilliantly. Army concerts sporadically appeared and invariably were rib ticklers. It was a relaxation during the afternoon to admire the beautiful gardens. Even a look around the cemetery was fascinating. The graves were elaborate mementoes with photographs of the loved ones imprinted in stone. Obviously costs were not curtailed and a French influence was clearly involved.

On the 8th December a few Moslem crew members said prayers, followed by their seasonal religious festivities. They had purchased a live sheep and poultry for the occasion. Unfortunately, the sight of the slow slitting of the animals' throats and their ritual death was not pleasant to our western eyes. I felt that the first chicken which they killed, died a slow, cruel death. Whereupon, I volunteered my expertise to despatch the next bird by immediate dislocation of its neck. The startled Muslims almost dislocated my neck, since in my ignorance, I had desecrated their fowl. It had to be replaced immediately by a fresh bird or **my** breathing would be stopped!

Since Christmas was fast approaching, our 1st mate built a poultry coop on deck to house our fresh birds in readiness. Christmas Day arrived and the cook took a chicken and literally swung it by its head in the belief that he was wringing its neck. It was a truly distressing exhibition of murder- more like swinging the starting handle of a car.

My memory could not have been as great as my conceit, because I volunteered to kill the next bird. I was relieved that I killed it, by dislocation of its neck, in under a second. It was exhibition stuff and it lured me on to attempt to kill the large turkey stag. As luck would have it, the bird was despatched rapidly and painlessly. Thus another expert kill was demonstrated. I always had the feeling thereafter that nobody was keen to have me walk behind him in the dark!

Christmas Day was a splendid affair with excellent food right up to the Christmas pudding, coffee and liqueurs. Then followed toasts to the King, the Navy,(to wives and sweethearts- may they never meet). There followed a separate toast to wives and then one to sweethearts. The numbers rising to each of these toasts gradually diminished, until only the sensible survived: the rest were insensible. I imagine if I had written up the log it would have read "Christmas enjoyed in true seafaring style."

We were loaded and sailed off to Gibraltar to pick up our convoy. The "Rock," known affectionately as "Gib." is a symbol of power guarding the Straits and we felt despite its recent bombardment in 1942, it would be held whatever the cost. It was the anchorage for Aircraft Carriers, Cruisers, Destroyers and the Royal Navy fighting ships. Apart from the Royal Naval base it was also much used by the Merchant Navy for convoy gathering and the MN. ships supplied food and equipment to the shore establishments.

The British first got a foothold on Gibraltar in 1702 when Royal Marines stormed the Rock and 1713 with the Treaty of Utrecht it was finally ceded to British control. A cable car took us to the `Top of the Rock' where the Barbary primates scampered about with great dexterity. Legend has it, that so long as these monkeys are on the Rock then the British will rule. The British garrison has NCOs designated to feed, water and look after the welfare of these rock apes. Thus symbolism and sentimentality are all part of this magnificent sentinel.

The commanding views are breathtaking not only of the Straits but right across the Mediterranean to the Moroccan coast. Gibraltar is a microcosm of the British way of life, including British Bobbies, fish'n chips and the changing of the guard. Both English and Spanish are spoken, English Pounds or Gibraltar Pounds are currency whilst prices are shown in pounds and pesetas.

The chambers of St Michael's Cave are used as a hospital. Care has to be taken with the catchment of water which is in short supply on Gibraltar. Finally, as we shopped we purchased a quantity of bananas and we hoped that they would keep in good condition and revive some memories for our folks back home.

Our convoy was now available so the brief run ashore terminated and it was back to war with our cargo of iron ore. This is a strange cargo because when the ship is fully laden the holds are still half empty. Consequently, if the hull is holed by torpedo or bomb the ship rapidly fills with water and disappears in under two minutes. To sink 'like a stone' is not as quick as 'like an iron ore ship.' A further consequence of this dead weight cargo is that the ship rolls with the cargo acting as a weighted pendulum. Thus the sailing motion becomes a constant slow rolling from side to side. Even on a calm sea, if the bow rises over a slight wave, this sets up a series of endless bobbing, up and down. If the weather is rough the reaction of the ship is to exaggerate every wave and be sluggishly slow to rise. Every year at least one ship carrying iron ore is lost. I can think of three in 1995 and of course the "Derbyshire" had iron ore as her cargo. Altogether, it rates as the third most dangerous cargo. Only High Octane and Amatol ammunition cargoes I would rate as more hazardous in circumstances of war. I am sure that the superstitious can now point to the reasons which were background for our present predicament!

Just through the Straits and heading north we were in the area known to sailors as "Hell's Alley." Our entry into "Hell's Alley" was confirmed by the arrival of Stukas attacking overhead. They flew in low from the sun and we held our breath as each plane appeared and closed. Although there were several planes attacking we seemed to single out one at a time. Especially targeted was the one which had chosen our ship for its victim and we retaliated accordingly. Our small convoy battled furiously but several successive waves of bombers came in, even their machine guns spraying vengeance. The gunner at our Oerlikon was shot and when I saw his anti aircraft gun swinging free, I grabbed it in a desperate effort to defend ourselves.

Miraculously I survived and later, as I looked around my feet at the spent shell cases, I picked up half a dozen as souvenirs. These I soldered together to form a pencil holder and this now has a prominent place beside our telephone and performs its useful purpose as well as being a momento of that occasion, which was my 20th Birthday.

———oOo———

4

MAIDEN VOYAGE

Inevitably, whilst I was appreciating the delights of being at home on leave, another telegram arrived. Another recall, which preceded another ship and of course another voyage, with no inkling as to which corner of the world I was destined. Variety is the spice of life and the appointed ship was no exception it was **SS EMPIRE STUART** 8000 Grt. managed by F.C.Strick & Co of London, and she was built in Shorts Yard at Sunderland. I signed articles on 4th February 1944 for her maiden voyage.

When signing articles at the shipping office, I was interested in the question, "Will you be willing to volunteer for " **D.Day"** to undertake any task required of you?" Willingness meant working on deck, the engine room, or in any capacity whatever need might arise. Paramount with our generation was a sense of duty. My belief was that I was involved in the defence of Freedom. I was also nurtured by the writings of Robert Burns, *A MAN'S A MAN FOR A' THAT.*

...... "The man o' independent mind"
and
...... "That man to man the world o'er,
Shall brithers be for a' that."

I did have my independence and choice. The question was therefore *courage* or *cowardice!* Thus I volunteered to undertake any task required of me and my identity card was stamped with a " V." Perhaps it was surprising but not everyone was prepared to venture thus far; proof that there was an element of choice. We were all well aware that the invasion build up had rapidly advanced to

EMPIRE STUART. 8,000 Grt. F.C. Strick & CO. Sailed Maiden Voyage to St John, Canada. Crippled, lost convoy, but limped back to dock in the Clyde.

the stage when it was almost imminent. It appeared we could be loading this time for the big push.

All "Empire Ships" were built in the UK. to a standard design. Their rapid construction was an effort to replace our heavy shipping losses. War time manufacture of most items produced a basic utility article, whether it was clothing, household furniture or ships. The *ss.Empire Stuart* was no exception. She was a standard simple steamship and she had not yet been sea rinsed. She was brand new and looked absolutely splendid.

The way to a sailor's heart could be via the cook. Our cook was excellent. In fact, as he was an experienced chef we had a happy ship. The Chief Radio Officer was an old timer and had been at sea long enough to become eccentric. His peculiarities involved a creativity which had become obsessional. At all times he was fully occupied, primarily, with carpentry. Before land had dipped below the horizon, he had made a switchboard, a tool rack, an ash tray and repaired a stool. He was compulsively engrossed in construction, but to feed his hobby he sought a constant supply of wood. Sneaking ashore he could be seen appropriating timber from the dockside, an action almost bordering on theft. This was not my problem, until I had to help him carry a plank twenty feet long, which we both had to struggle to lift on board as material to feed his passion for carpentry during the voyage.

I noticed that already there were pencil marks on it, where he had marked out the sections to be sawn. After all, a section of timber twenty feet by twelve inches by three inch thick is difficult to manipulate or hide. Quickly it was sawn into sections and stowed out of view in readiness for making the next piece of furniture which was soon underway. He was a travelling workshop with saw, chisels, brace and of course screwdrivers, electric iron and a typewriter. On his previous voyage he had been out East sailing in the same ship for three years. Thus he had avoided the standard routine of changing ships. He had thus accumulated a considerable amount of gear which would probably require a removal van rather than a mundane taxi whenever he changed ships.

We set off up the east coast with the customary call into Methil. Sometimes this involved bunkering or awaiting convoy but, realistically, it was a question of timing so that we arrived at the Pentland Firth with the appropriate tidal conditions.

According to "Reed's Nautical Almanac"

"The Pentland Firth probably represents the most difficult navigational passage on the Coasts of the United Kingdom, normally used by vessels of all sizes. Owing to the great strength of the Tidal Stream (more than the speed of the average small vessel) at times, the utmost care should be used, especially in thick weather or uncertain visibility. Study the tidal streams for safety's sake."

In some places the spring tidal rate reaches ten point five knots. That was faster than our maximum speed. Besides,since we were 'light'ship, the propeller was not fully submerged and thus we were losing thrust. Also, when a ship rides high out of the sea, considerable windage problems arise. Cape Wrath would be passed en route and doubtless there are hidden dangers to justify that title.

Dunnet Head lighthouse is on the summit of a 300 ft. cliff at the south-western entrance to the Pentland Firth and its windows have been broken repeatedly. The raging sea sweeps stones from the cliff and thrusts them up against the lighthouse. These warnings are sufficient to make a navigator's adrenaline run vigorously as he plots the ship's course round the north of Scotland.

The "Bore of Duncansby" and the "Merry Men of Mey" rage at opposite ends of the Pentland Firth. Smaller vessels are cautioned to batten down the hatches because the transition from smooth water to broken sea is so sudden that no time is given for making arrangements. It is not surprising therefore that Masters of vessels in Loch Ewe or Methil take note of tide and weather conditions before proceeding North about. These are some of the factors which doubtless encouraged the construction of the Caledonian Canal.

In passing, whilst on the subject of "tide" it is interesting to observe that sailors and fishermen believe that the flood tide indicates strength, and that the ebb tide portrays weakness. Thus when an old salt is seriously ill his family will watch the tide. If he survives the ebb then he is expected to improve on the flood. It is likely, one presumes, that he would die on the ebb. In which case one might find an epitaph "He went out with the tide and sunset."

Weather forecasting for holiday makers on the coast take heed:

If it rains on the ebb go back to bed,
If it rains on the flow get up, and go.

Before setting off from Methil, I was able to obtain a library of books from The War Library Service. As one can imagine this was a godsend, and as self appointed ship's librarian, I anticipated being pleasantly occupied during the voyage. It was time to set off north about Scottish waters and through the Pentland Firth to Loch Ewe. If one recalls one's Shakespeare:

There is a tide in the affairs of men,
Which, taken at the flood, leads on to fortune.
                              (Julius Caesar 1V iii)

On arrival, Loch Ewe had an ominous air as it was dark and moody which somehow foretold all would not be well when we ventured forth. But it was winter and February was not the brightest of months to anchor on a deep, sultry loch, surrounded by those stern hills. The hour of departure arrived and slowly we steamed out into the Atlantic to meet our convoy. We anticipated that it would be a rough crossing. It was winter and in the North Atlantic a ship would be expected to pitch and roll. Even so, we surpassed every angle of heel possible, short of turning turtle. We rolled one side under water and then swinging back the opposite bulwark was completely submerged. The sea cascaded over the side of the ship and flooded the decks repeatedly. We probably would have swung a clinometer off its bearings. Sleeping was disturbed by the pressures of trying to remain wedged in my bunk as this ship rolled prodigiously. Pillows were placed on the lee side with my knees wedged against the lee board in an endeavour to avoid being tipped out of bed.

We were rolling violently and heeling so far over, that within the first week at sea, all of our life-rafts had been lost from both sides of the ship. Each measured about 24ft x 12ft. and we had set off with four brand new rafts on board as our emergency life-saving equipment. They were capable of floating upside down because the air tanks were in the centre and they were equally suitable either side up. The rafts were held at a fixed angle of forty-five degrees supported on steel cradles. They were firmly secured by chain and a quick release mechanism. Lifeboats often cannot be lowered when torpedoed because the ship probably has developed a list and a lifeboat would simply drop on to the side of the hull. The opposite side of the ship, where she was holed and suffered the explosion, would be likely to have lifeboats damaged and unusable. Thus these rafts were supposed to remedy such circumstances and save lives when abandoning ship. We had already rolled ours overboard which left us exposed and vulnerable.

As we proceeded our problems mounted. One of the derricks broke loose from its holding crutch. These heavy steel derricks were fifty foot long and resembled metal telegraph poles. As the ship rolled from side to side this free swinging monster shattered or bent everything it struck. Steel steps leading down to the deck were torn free and rapidly demolished. Iron ladders were wrenched off the bulkhead and the heavy metal pole then battered the hatch tops into submission until their splintered remains offered us little protection from the cascading seas. Try tying down that flying monster, on a ship alternately rolling its sides under. It was a herculean task fraught with danger but lives had to be risked in an attempt. Seamen don't shirk dangerous situations and this was yet another which demanded their skills. It was also a factor which could determine the ship's survival. Atlantic seas in winter are formidable enough without the might of a rogue derrick wrecking the ship.

In the main saloon the furniture looked beautiful with our new cushioned armchairs set around the dining table. Underneath the seat of each chair, a spring connection secured it to a `U' bolt fixed into the deck. Unfortunately, as the ship rolled and extra pressure was put on this spring, it would suddenly expand and break loose. The person still sitting on the chair careered backwards across the saloon floor to finally crash into the rear bulkhead. The victim, bruised and groaning was more fortunate than the chair, since he at least survived in one piece. The chairs and their attractive curved arms shattered on impact. Either the legs, arms or both were broken. Before reaching Canada most of this beautiful furniture was reduced to matchwood. Splintered remains soon piled high in the corner of the saloon as witness to the repeated failure of these flimsy fixtures. Scarcely a chair survived the outward passage without serious damage.

If that had been the extent of our problems one might have overlooked these mishaps as the expectations of a maiden voyage. However, at midnight the relief watch failed to appear on the bridge. Investigators going down aft to the crew quarters found them trapped under collapsed bunks. On that occasion nobody was injured other than severe bruising but these breakages occurred too frequently for complacency. Several fittings were not robust enough to withstand the impositions of the rough seas and it was particulary annoying when the bunk lee boards sprung loose.

As a ship rolls the occupant of the bunk puts his full weight on to the bunk board on his lee side. He leans on to it as he tries to avoid being tipped out. The screw fastenings used on the *Empire Stuart* were obviously inadequate since they failed to retain the bunk boards. The sleeping occupant was fortunate if he avoided breaking a limb as he fell out through the air. One could guarantee that hitting the deck awakened even those deepest in slumber, provided they escaped being knocked out in the process.

Our rolling was excessive and that could not be disputed. It was suggested that this was due to insufficient ballast in the ship. It involved both time and expense to load materials and of course there was very little ballast material which could be spared for export from Britain at that time. Thus it was perhaps expedient to overlook ballasting. On the otherhand many wartime ships may have lacked ballast but few had to suffer such damage as we encountered.

ST.JOHN

St.John, New Brunswick, in the Bay of Fundy, could have been more welcoming but the weather was desperately cold. Every stitch of clothing had to be worn, including pyjamas, in an effort to find comfort. Bottles of beer froze solid. Grapefruit congealed to resemble iron cannon balls. Ice built up inside the cabin bulkheads until there was no escape from the intense cold. How wonderful it would have been to have had somewhere on the ship sufficiently warm just to thaw out.

It is strange to reflect that this region is further South than Britain. The difference in temperatures is due to the cold Labrador current compared to our Gulf Stream. We were not adequately prepared to withstand the extremely cold conditions either in our cabins or elsewhere on board ship. We were young and fit so it went down as experience. Later when I suffered the extremes of heat in the Red Sea I reflected fondly upon our freeze up in St.John.

Repairing some of the damage to the ship delayed our departure. This was a splendid opportunity to view the famous natural wonders of the "Reversing Falls, at the mouth of the "Saint John River". Twice daily the force of the water as it pounds into the Bay causes the river to flow **backwards.** It is a spectacular phenomenon particularly if witnessed on a spring tide. I was able to capitalise on our extra free time by sight seeing. It was interesting to venture out to see the curious "Flower Pot Rocks" in the Bay of Fundy. These amazing rock structures have been sculpted by the highest tides in the world. Yet again the tides fascinate us as this formidable force has left these mysterious pinnacle rocks with their verdant tops which can even be seen sporting a flourishing tree.

Further sights worth observation were the twenty species of whales in the Bay: finback, minke, humpback and also Atlantic white-sided dolphin together with harbour porpoise. Certainly our delayed start was not time wasted. I regarded it as a bonus opportunity not to be squandered.

"Exultation is the going" Emily Dickinson 1830-1886.

> *Exultation is the going*
> *Of an inland soul to sea,*
> *Past the houses-past the headlands-*
> *Into deep Eternity-*
> *Bred as we, among the mountains,*
> *Can the sailor understand*
> *The divine intoxication*
> *Of the first league out from land? ...*

The answer, dear Emily, is "Yes." In fact, when a sailor is ashore it does not take long before he is finding himself "seasick" and pining to be afloat. After a short spell ashore, "Exultation" is what he invariably feels with the first league out from land and a fresh sea breeze. Thus was I exalted to be on our way again back to the

UK. The motion of the ship was markedly subdued due to the weight of her cargo as she was fully laden. Rolling and pitching yes, but this time with the exhilaration of the forebitter shanty:

>*"Rolling home, rolling home,*
>*Rolling home across the sea,*
>*Rolling home to dear old Scotland,*
>*Rolling home, dear land, to thee."*

This was the voyage now, to debunk that old taboo which sailors have when they show little enthusiasm for a maiden voyage. They say that the first trip is surely for cleansing the ship of the ill-luck accumulated during building.

I was pleasantly occupied with these thoughts, or was I just tempting fate? Suddenly, without any warning **ss.Empire Stuart** with a will of her own started to swerve off course.
"Watch it, quartermaster! **Watch it!**"
"Sorry Sir, she`s gone...not answering the helm!"
Quick, two blasts on the siren. We are swinging to port.
The first mate tugged at the chain to sound the ship`s whistle. There was no response. The chain dropped loose as it broke and pulled apart.

Call the Captain!

The ship was out of control so the telegraph was rung "Stop Engines!" Slowly we were losing way as the ship slowed down, but our problem was the ship astern.She was just visible in the gloom of early morning as dawn had not yet broken.
The captain appeared on the bridge and yelled, **"Lights!"**
The two emergency vertical red lights were switched on to indicate out of control. They did not come on. Repeatedly the switches were pushed but they were completely dead. There was no response!

We were now at the mercy of the ship astern which was appearing at normal speed and it looked as if we would be ploughed down. It depended on the vigilance on the other ship. Would our plight be seen in time to take avoiding action? Darkness cloaks vessels without lights into spectres and black shapes almost not discernible until it is too late.

At last, frantic figures were visible, darting across her bridge. Almost just in time, she was starting to swing to starboard. Was she going to miss? It did not look as though she could turn out of the way quickly enough to avoid collision. We were still swinging slightly and she was turning slowly in the opposite direction.

Would we collide? Would we miss? Our sides touched then rubbed together, sparks flying, paint searing hot. The acrid smell and sudden heat generated made one thank the stars that we were not a volatile vessel. Then a slight roll apart and the great lumbering mass swept past with no more damage than dents, paintwork and our bent bulwark.

One more ship has yet to pass. Shall we still be lucky? We await anxiously, eyes straining to pick out her ominous shape. There she is coming now! One could just see the image firming up out of the gloom but she seems gigantic! Things happen quickly when disaster impends. We shall be sinking or fighting to survive in a matter of the next few minutes. We had drifted slightly out of our line so that now there was a little more space for the oncoming vessel to hold course and almost pass. It looked more hopeful. If only they can see us in time to take some avoiding action. Yes, there she goes, starting her turn to starboard.

We watched as she grew to her enormous full size, with her frothing bow wave churning towards us. The bow, coming up on our stern, was only twenty feet apart but still turning away. We watched the monster thrust her way past, but of course she was dragged towards us by the increased speed of the sea separating the two ships. We were drawn together with only inches to spare. We struck, rubbed, scraped and intermittently rolled apart with damage amounting to bends and dents. The danger surged, then passed, with our damage as witness but nothing too serious. It was a scary episode, more startling for the Captain who overall bore the responsibility of this wayward unco-operative vessel. He could have been forgiven had he retired to his cabin to seek fortification for his buffeted nervous system but we were still in a dangerous situation. Only last night we had lost a ship from the convoy through enemy action. This was not a time to be alone and stationary. Anxiety showed on the faces of the crew and there was a quivering nervousness that could only be dispelled when we were again under way. It took most of the day to rig an emergency form of steering since our hydraulic system had completely collapsed and could not be restored. There was no hope of rejoining the convoy as it had long since disappeared from view. We were on our own , a straggler, our only chance now was to proceed with all speed to reach the North passage before being sighted by a U-Boat.

The engineers and crew struggled all morning and it was late afternoon before trials could be carried out to see if the jury rig would work. We used the drums of the steam deck winches to wind cable on the starboard side, the port side having first been slackened off. Then slackening the starboard cable the port winch would pull. It was important to first have the slack as otherwise the strain could snap the wire hawser and that would spell disaster for whoever might be in its path. One crew member was stationed on the starboard winch and another on the port.
It took a lot of practice to co-ordinate this operation. I never thought that I would see a cargo vessel tacking its course across the ocean. First we would swing to starboard. A few miles later an effort was made to recover the distance by steering on a port tack. We were 500 miles from the Mull of Kintyre. We sent a radio message to summon a tug because there was just no way we could steer through the North Channel. It is fifteen miles distance

between the Mull of Kintyre and Northern Ireland. This gap was too narrow for the erratic steering controls we were using.

The good news was that we would be docking at my home port on the Clyde. The necessary repairs to the *Empire Stuart* would be undertaken on the Clyde. Thereafter, she participated in the invasion of "D-day." Meantime, of course, I had to move on. Marconi did not allow any slack time and wherever possible our position as sailors took precedence over the opportunity of being landlubbers. I did not have the choice of waiting until repairs were completed otherwise I could have been included in the D-day invasion. Such is the hand of fate.

5

CROSSING ATLANTIC IN STYLE

RMS.QUEEN MARY. *(Grey Ghost)*
It was sheer delight to have docked on the Clyde so near home. I managed to call on the family immediately on arrival, even before signing off. Also I circumvented the running around, administration and travelling. It was absolutely fabulous and extended my leave, almost doubling the time ashore with my folks. It was a short trip, followed by a short leave and I went back to sea within the week. However, since I was reporting to the local Marconi office in Glasgow, there was the likelihood that I could sail from the Clyde.

Meantime, it was great to be at home with family and link up again with friends and relations. It is terribly important, especially in conditions of war, stress or a prolonged period spent abroad, to have the anchor of a home and family. Perhaps this is more so if the homing instinct is strong and love of country deep and meaningful:

> *....Breathes there a man with soul so dead*
> *Who never to himself hath said*
> *This is my own, my native land!*
> *Whose heart hath ne'er within him burned,*
> *As home his footsteps he hath turned*
> *From wandering on a foreign strand?...*
> *Sir.W.Scott.*

I am happy to find myself with these strengths or weaknesses depending upon one's point of view. At least I have always felt that such an anchor is sustaining, particularly where circumstances are difficult. Always there is the satisfaction that something wonderful awaits the termination of one's deprivation. Furthermore being an optimist or having a rooted belief in the future is a winning formula.

My batteries were recharged nicely by the few days leave and I was then ready for whatever fortune rolled up on the dice. What a slice of luck it was too; Dame Fortune threw me a double six! I was directed to board the "Queen Mary." I could not have imagined being ever so fortunate! This was unbelievable and the fulfilment of a dream spawned on that day when I first witnessed her launch.

The **QUEEN MARY** now a legend of the Atlantic! I could recollect her shining black hull, brilliant white superstructure and three raked red funnels with her striking black tops to add a final touch of dignity. Seeing her beautiful lines and cruiser stern, I just could not wait to board this magnificent vessel. I was directed to Greenock where the great ship was anchored off shore at the tail of the bank. I would be ferried out to her by a local passenger steamer.

It was amazing, but I had forgotten that she was now described as the *Grey Ghost* There she lay, still **RMS.QUEEN MARY** the super-liner, but overall she was now painted in her wartime grey. Thus she had thwarted the prize of 250,000 dollars and the iron cross offered to the U-boat commander who could torpedo this great prize. Evasion was due to her being the world's fastest ship and holder of the blue ribbon. Also, as she sailed across the Atlantic she executed a zigzag course and could outrun her frustrated enemies as she darted across at thirty knots.

The building of this giant ship will always be regarded as a triumph of imagination and skill. She measured 1018 Ft.long with 118 Ft. beam. 81,000 Grt. Keel to masthead 234 Ft. The Nelson monument 170 ft tall would leave Nelson's hat no higher than her boat deck.

At the outbreak of war she was in New York and for a period thought to be too valuable and too large a target to risk at sea. Then the decision was taken for her to voyage to Australia to be converted for troop carrying. She initially took 5,000 troops but further conversion, for cooler Atlantic voyaging, resulted in conveying 8,500 troops per crossing. Churchill said that her great contribution (with her sister ship Queen Elizabeth) meant that the war had been shortened by one year. Soon after the end of the war she conveyed 22,000 American war brides returning to the United States to their new husbands. She had travelled 650,000 miles and made 1,001 Atlantic crossings without loss of lives to the enemy. She is undoubtedly a legend and the World's favourite liner.

When she sailed into New York on her maiden voyage, aeroplanes came out to greet this great lady. Then as she entered the river every boat that could float came out to give her a rapturous welcome. Craft virtually choked the river. Each boat had its whistle tied down and the tremendous cacophony of sound was indescribable. Everyone in New York and beyond packed the river banks and folks took the day off work in order not to miss seeing this great liner dock at pier ninety.

To travel on this village afloat, was an incredible experience. Apart from her tremendous size, the luxurious accommodation and fittings, even when stripped for war, were opulent. The ballroom was elegant and spacious with its maple wood floor. The first class smoke room had a log burning fire. The observation lounge and dining rooms with exquisite wood carvings, astonishing murals, sculpted friezes and furnishings all contributed to a nautical extravaganza. There was even a shopping centre, banking, hairdressing and beauty salon. It is little wonder that its central area was known as "Piccadily Circus."

Merchant ships pre-war had one wireless operator. The Queen Mary had eight operators and two radio stations separated by a distance of 250ft. to permit simultaneous transmission without interference. The volume of radio telegraphic and radio telephonic work on a vessel of this size was tremendous. Four transmitters enabled communications to be maintained with both sides of the Atlantic. Some thirty wavelengths were required, nine separate aerial systems with the main aerial having a 600ft span. Public broadcasting within the ship enabled different music to be relayed to suit the various demands from orchestral to dance. Telephone calls could also be made from any one of the 500 state rooms.

The promenade deck was tremendous fun and a jolly good hike for the energetic. On my voyage, she was rock steady, hence the reason for furnishings not being secured in any way. However, this was not invariably so and the power of the Atlantic was under estimated yet again. On one voyage she rolled to forty-four degrees, which meant to walk, one had to have one foot on the wall and the other on the deck, since she was half way from the vertical.

Likewise when she rolled to and fro a thick pile carpet in the lounge followed and so did the furnishings. In the tourist lounge an upright piano charged hither and thither for days wrecking everything in its path including itself. Only an iron frame survived in the shambles but it was a twanging harping orchestration of destruction. Nobody dared enter to stop this melee since it was too dangerous. I believe after that trip twenty-seven ambulances awaited on the quay to collect the injured passengers. She was subsequently fitted with stabilisers to cure this oversight.

One wartime disaster occurred when she was being escorted by the cruiser **HMS Curacao** approaching Scotland. The cruiser sailed across in front of the **Queen Mary** and was sliced in two, sinking in under two minutes, with a loss of 329 out of her crew of 430. The damage to the **Queen Mary** was only superficial, such

RMS. QUEEN MARY. Cunard White Star liner. 81,000 GRT. 26th September 1935 launched Clyde
I had to run backwards to avoid the wash. 20th Apl. 1944 sailed on *Grey Ghost* zig/zag 30knts N.YK.

was the strength of her construction.

It would be ungracious not to mention the cuisine. Travelling first class we had seven courses of delectable nutrients and to feed all the troops it took seven sittings per meal. The service, dare I say, was absolutely impeccable. I doubt if ever I had better fare.

Passenger ships always have at least one outstanding person who becomes the focus of attention. On this occasion it was a uniquely stylish lady. She would stroll along the promenade deck with a handbag under her arm and a soft posterior wobbling with seductive intent. She was dressed in what Sir Winston Churchill launched as the "Siren Suit." This was similar to a boiler suit but of expensive material and the ideal apparel for emergency wear in air raids. The lady in this fashionable outfit, wore expensive furs draped over her shoulders forming a stylish cape and her head was shrouded in a designer turban.

When we had a show produced by the passengers on the stage in the theatre, she appeared! Not in person, but mimicked, as walking across the stage with her handbag, of course. Well, no script was needed, the entire audience collapsed in convulsions in the funniest few minutes that could possibly be contrived. Yet it did become more hilarious because the debunked lady herself appeared remonstrating at the front of the stage. The laughter was uproarious and too noisy to distinguish whether she was hurling obscenities at the actor, who with suitable affectations strutted off the stage. Then, adding insult to injury, the actor again walked out from the other side of the stage pulling a toy Donald Duck along behind him. It took five minutes for this extra wave of laughter to subside.

We also had deck games, parties, entertainment and almost marriages. Amazing bonds were formed within this artificial world of four days. Possibly it's the close togetherness that causes these magnetic attractions, or perhaps Cupid was on the passenger list?

Southampton had been her home port and when she sailed out for the last time with 165,000 HP engines driving her giant propellers and the magic sound of her droning whistle, it was a very emotional event. It was experienced by thousands upon thousands who came to line the shores of southern England for the sad last sight of their favourite liner.

She is now berthed at Long Beach, California as a floating hotel and conference centre, a show piece viewed by millions of nostalgic passengers, ex-servicemen, and visitors each year. She is now as much part of Long Beach as the Eiffel Tower is of Paris. Mention Long Beach and everyone will remark, "Oh, that is where the *Queen Mary* is berthed." An unforgettable ship, she towers overall.

When we berthed at New York and stepped ashore from the *Queen Mary* a band played to welcome American servicemen in particular but as we were in uniform we were included. Girls served doughnuts, a glass of milk, cookies, or coffee with unbounded hospitality. Uncle Sam`s boys are paid respect and Americans do appreciate and look after their heroes.

There was a bus laid on to convey us to the Wentworth Hotel at 59 West 46th Street,N.Y. It was fantastic to be down-town and soak up the atmosphere of this city. Manhattan, Bronx, Queens, and Brooklyn were all within easy subway hops.

At night, Times Square, Broadway and various shows had our patronage. During the days with the hotel as our base,Central Park and even Coney Island had our attention as tourists. In fact, when we went to Coney Island, I made my first parachute jump at one of the fun fair installations. It is amazing what one will do as a stunt for bravado, I think it was pride which was my downfall! Just my luck, that I was in the USA. where Americans boast that everything which they own is either the biggest or the best. On this latter point I now declined to agree.

Soon, I was appointed to take charge of some members of the crew and to board the train for Savannah. We had first class accommodation reserved in "Pullman Cars" for the overnight eighteen hour journey. This was an opportunity to exchange the city streets for fine glimpses of this vast country's landscape.

The observation car demonstrated the friendly characteristics of our American passengers. There was no reticence here and I had to respond to enquiries about my uniform, my voyages and to explain the life of a sailor. Eventually, I found myself the centre of attraction. It became almost like being on stage holding forth, especially when they heard that I had sailed on a Danish ship and on an Estonian ship. How did I cope with the language and what was the food like? Unfortunately, as they don't converse in whispers other passengers overhearing my replies joined in. It soon seemed apparent that a local radio station might find me a suitable candidate for a broadcast and would ask to interview me. At that point I made a strategic withdrawal.

Then there was the incident of the guy who felt that he had been bitten repeatedly by bugs and could not sleep. He wrote a strong letter of complaint to the "Pullman Authorities." He received an indignant reply about how preposterous to even suggest the presence of bugs in such hygienic conditions as offered by "Pullman Cars." It was impossible, simply out of the question. The passenger felt that, perhaps, after all he had been mistaken, until a hand-written slip of paper fell out of the envelope on which was written"Send this guy the bug letter!"

———oOo———

6

THE LIBERTY SHIP

The Savannah hotel Georgia was a delightful spot in which to savour southern hospitality. We had several days' shore comforts before embarking on our new ship. Relaxation was to meander along the palm tree lined roads of this small town and enjoy the park areas shaded from the hot southern sun. Of course, we had only a few days to enjoy the temperatures and reduced tempo from city life. Then we boarded the *SS. SAMCEBU.* The ship had the prefix "SAM" indicating "Superstructure Aft of Midship." Often one finds the suggestion that because these ships were built in the U.S.A . it is a reference to "Uncle Sam," but that is not so.

In December 1940 Churchill wrote to President Roosevelt about shipping replacements pointing out the necessity to be able to feed our Island, import munitions, and be able to move our armies by sea. I quote his remarks in that letter. *It is therefore in shipping and in the power to transport across oceans, particularly the Atlantic Ocean, that in 1941 the crunch of the whole war will be found.*

Churchill's "Second World War, volume 2" came out in 1949 and included his comments about the above letter reflecting that *The letter, which was one of the most important I ever wrote...*it also demonstrates the remarkable foresight shown by Churchill where he anticipates the course of the war.

The letter persuaded President Roosevelt that there was an urgent need to build cargo vessels to help redress our losses. In due course our ships were being sunk at a rate which was five times faster than replacements could be built. The American response was to supply us with the ' Liberty' ships which were transferred to Britain on Lease\Lend terms and had the prefix "Sam" in their name. The *Samcebu* was the one on which I sailed.

Initially the Americans had neither the ships available nor the shipyards in which they could be built. R.Cyril Thompson, of Sunderland shipbuilders, went out to the States taking with him the plans of the *Empire Liberty* which was the first emergency war time ship built in Sunderland. These plans were a great help in providing the rapid start to building which was vitally necessary.

In the absence of available shipyards we financed and organised the building of two yards, one in California and one in Portland Maine. Sixty ships were ordered, thirty from each of these yards and they were named "Ocean" starting with the *Ocean Vanguard.* A further twenty-six were built in Canadian yards and they were prefixed with the name "Fort." The Americans subsequently bought both yards from us. They built new facilities and from a total of eighteen yards they soon produced the phenomenal output of the 'Liberty Ship' as an "emergency standard" cargo carrier. Whilst returning to Britain in December 1940 Cyril Thompson was torpedoed on the *Western Prince* but he survived and managed to get all the plans and the signed agreement documents back safely to Britain.

The *SS. SAMCEBU* was a ' Liberty Ship' and we had the privilege of sailing her back to the UK. on her *maiden voyage.* She was 10,865 dead-weight tons, 441 ft. x 57 ft. & draft 27ft. Liberty Ships based on the simple British design more than proved their worth, because despite their failings, 2710 were built to quickly redress our losses in the Battle of the Atlantic. It would be no exaggeration to say that the prolific production of these ships changed the course of the war. They may be accredited with saving not only Britain and the Allied cause but probably the whole world from disaster. Their largely welded construction enabled three ships to be launched each day. The quickest on record took only four days, fifteen hours thirty minutes from keel laying to launching. Such speedy construction was made possible by **welding** large **sub-assemblies** elsewhere then bringing them together for final assembly. Both of these techniques were innovative for ship building. The reward was a staggering output in the U.S.A. which was quite phenomenal.

If, however, one analyses the work rate, in terms of output per man hour, one finds that British Shipyards excelled by a ratio of 2:1. Our workers achieved the equivalent output in only half the time. In America the labour force was practically unlimited thus many more shipyard workers were employed and they certainly launched more ships than we could possibly attain.

These ships were said to split open sometimes and this weakness was analysed by *Constance Tipper* a metallurgist at the Cambridge Low Temperature Research Unit, England. She developed the "Tipper Test" to determine the vulnerability of steel at low temperatures. This was crucial in the understanding of why Liberty Ships split open in rough seas. The sudden cooling of the welding produced a brittle factor in its crystalline structure. These ships were prone to this problem especially when they were built during the cool winter months in the U.S.A. When 'light' ship, the "Liberties" rode high out of the water with the propeller whipping round only half submerged, so that considerable power was lost.

In April 1947 the Liberty ship *Samtampa* was on her way to the Bristol Channel. The weather as she came north from Landsend became horrendous. The Radio Officer of another ship picked up her anguished call for help. The *Samtampa* turned around and with her engines full ahead, she tried to fight back against wind and sea. Both anchors were dropped and for a moment there was some hope. Then one anchor gave way, followed shortly by the other. Now she was being blown backwards on to the rocks at

SS.SAMCEBU. 7,176 Grt. Liberty Ship Maiden Voyage from Savanah to U.K. May 1944.

Sker Point at the mouth of the Bristol Channel. The Mumbles lifeboat went to her aid but both lifeboat and ship foundered with all hands.

The difficulties of insufficient ballast conjures up the idea that there should be a "Light Loadline" for ships. Whilst this might be true, particularly of Liberty ships, they are by no means the only ones with this shortcoming. Fortunately, we made our Atlantic crossing without splitting open and we avoided being another statistic with the fifty known Liberty Ships which were lost through enemy action on their maiden voyage. Altogether Liberty ship war casualties exceeded two hundred.

I had the opportunity of boarding a Liberty Ship, the *Jeremiah O`Brien,* when she attended the 50th Anniversary Commemoration of "D.DAY" in June 1994. It was a salutary reminder to see her dull grey hull and drab war time austerity. There was no bright work (glistening varnish) and no polished brass. The front of the bridge and the external bulkhead of the radio room were protected with special plastic armament since these were the vulnerable targeted areas. The windows on the front of the bridge were mere narrow safeguarded slits. She was preserved for posterity unaltered from her war time condition which included her guns and liferafts in position. The stark utility of our war time environment, completely lacking any colour, now surprised me. I had almost forgotten that we had endured a dull sullen existence and this was a grim reminder of my past wartime experience. Also it demonstrated the depths of deprivation imposed by fighting that war. How strange, in retrospect, to think back on those times and even to recall that **only black** cars were available in the UK.and that they had cans, with slits in them over the headlamps, as a blackout precaution.

The Americans have proudly preserved two of their Liberty Ships, but only one, the *Jeremiah O`Brien,* attended the celebrations at the anniversary of the 'D.Day' invasion. She now serves as a living tribute to the men and women who built and sailed these ships. Twenty-five per cent of the builders or more could be women and this again was a record. The vintage triple expansion engine of this ship was seen running several times in the recently released "Titanic" film.

A group of Merchant Marine Veterans are involved in the USA., helping to save the Liberty Ship for posterity and as a memorial to merchant seamen who served in World War Two. Both the John W Brown and the Jeremiah O'Brien were brought up to standard and are operated by volunteers, who serve without pay or compensation. In the USA. they are regarded as National Treasures. The John W Brown is berthed at Baltimore and the National Liberty Ship Memorial of Jeremiah O'Brien has a permanent berth at San Francisco.

——oOo——

7

TRUE FRIENDSHIP

... God gives all men all earth to love
But since man`s heart is small
Ordains for each one spot shall prove
Beloved over all. ...
                    Kipling. "Sussex."

However fond one is of homeland, duty calls and after one week it
was back to war. I signed off the Liberty Ship at Liverpool and
was recalled to Liverpool. Not surprising, because this was Brit-
ain`s main convoy port throughout the six war years. An average
of three or four convoys arrived each week, with food and materiels of war, especially from Canada and U.S.A.   Apart from handling cargoes from all of these ships, Merseyside also built and repaired large numbers of warships and merchant ships.The head-
quarters of the Western Approaches Command, the nerve centre of
planning and organisation of the Battle of the Atlantic, was based
in Liverpool. Significantly, it was later combined H.Q. with an
R.A.F. component, so that eventually closer co-operation between
air and sea forces was possible. Western Approaches Command
conducted all convoy and anti submarine operations in the eastern
Atlantic. The Command was able to co-ordinate information
from the Submarine Tracking Room and Bletchley Park. Training
of naval groups was emphasised, so that initially inadequate forces
were made as effective tactically as possible. Overall the meas-
ures constituted the tactical battle which lead to our supremacy in
the Battle of the Atlantic.
Liverpool also suffered heavily from German air raids.

Her citizens in the docks and city were all active participants in the war effort. This port was a living fortress as could be seen by the number of Service Men and Women on its streets. The entire River Mersey and its Docks were bristling with ships and the multiplicity of so many vessels packing the river and port is unlikely ever to be matched again.

At Liverpool, I signed on articles for the *MV. LORETO* of the Pacific Steam Navigation Company. She measured 6,682 Grt. 406ft.x 54ft. The P.S.N.C. was a Royal Mail company and this was their smallest ship. A relatively small cargo passenger ship, she was capable of carrying twelve passengers. How sad it is, that we no longer have such gems afloat, whereby a short sea passage could nurture nostalgia. Her usual trading would be with South America. Overall the company had the aura of 'Royal Mail Classification' and thus had splendid passenger ships.

A rather pukka attitude pervaded the officer class but the victualling on the *mv. Loreto* did not match these superior airs. The excuse was that they had been unable to obtain stores when leaving the U.K. It was surprising the difference in quality of catering found in different ships. Some companies had meagre, if not sub standard fare, which earned them appalling reputations. One of the poorest companies, with dire consequences for those crew members with good appetites, was "Ropners." I remember when we had to attend a first aid lecture in Liverpool. In the lecture hall there were officers, stewards, cooks, A.B.'s (able bodied seamen) and crew, all awaiting instruction. The white coated doctor appeared on the stage, opened his wooden box and pulled out a skeleton. He held it aloft to the gathering and said "You all know what this is." A voice from the back of the hall called out, "An A.B. from Ropners!" Another company with two thick white bands around its funnel and with a thin red band between, was known as "Hungry Harrisons," two of fat and one of lean.

We had an incident with our junior Radio Officer when we entered tropical weather. We changed into our "whites"- white short sleeved shirt, white shorts or trousers and of course stockings and shoes. This was the young Radio Officer's first voyage and he was not as well kitted out as the more experienced. He did have white shorts and shirt but a message from the captain indicated that he was improperly dressed. Where were his epaulets? If he wished to dine in the saloon he must ensure that he was properly dressed!

Well, we got our heads together and made up a pair of epaulets out of cardboard and cloth with one gold braid zig zag line on each. They passed the test at a distance and although snobbery knows no bounds, he was tolerated. Other ships are at the other extreme and are lacking in etiquette, proving that every ship is a unique world of its own. What a pity the food on this voyage was the poorest so far encountered; rather than upper class it was inferior.

Our destination was the "States" which turned out to be Baltimore, Maryland. The first treasure found ashore was the Merchant Navy Club. Here we had the most wonderful entertainment. This was enhanced by melodious tones from a juke-box which had magical acoustics and lights which rippled across its front to dance in sympathy with the music. Some claim that sound reproduction has diminished in quality since glass valves were superseded by transistors. Possibly that subscribes to nostalgia but juke-boxes were in a world of their own with sound. I recall the round deep timbre with a resonance unmatched today. We absorbed those juke-box vibrations, enveloped by the total atmosphere and music of the forties. These tunes and lyrics have been imprinted for life. Several decades have slipped past but when that music is heard old pleasures of Baltimore are re-lived. "Begin the Beguine" the original version, tuned my formative years. That was the song which floated along with the flotsam of my teens to nurture the beginning of my adulthood.

We also enjoyed playing snooker each afternoon at the club and this was varied with table tennis. There was further entertainment partaken at the bar and on the dance-floor. Such skills were developed and their achievement proved very satisfying. As we spent several weeks in dry dock undertaking repairs, this backwater of peace was invaluable, being remote from the rust chipping hammers and riveters on board our ship and of course those tempestuous seas.

Night life tempted the naughty, which is a more honest description than nautical. There was the sleazy or to be frank, highly entertaining sailors' end of town. Young innocent sailors could learn much about life from a close study of the strip shows which offered a fully comprehensive education. Just before obtaining my degree in this entertainment, I was diverted by kindly hostesses calling at the M.N. Club.

The first lady asked if a couple of boys would like to come out of town for a picnic. This was typical American hospitality which we, being gallant, could not refuse. The chicken drumsticks and iced cocktails were served at umbrella-shaded tables set on a beautifully manicured lawn in a six acre garden. The lavish house and living style could have been from a film set. The glorious sunshine radiated a brilliant warmth which hovered around one hundred degrees Fahrenheit. Our comfort was further assured as a soft cooling breeze caressed our reclining leisured pose whilst the summery hostesses ensured that drinks, iced and alcoholic, added the extras to our enjoyment.

A gentleman called at the club one day, to ask if a couple of boys would like to join him at his country retreat. Why not? So Leslie and I were whisked off in his limousine. En route, we stopped as he purchased our ice cream which was gigantic! Then we saw a large truck-load of water melons which were on display by the roadside. Did we like them? Several were purchased for our appraisal. We were discussing the crop in the fields which apparently was corn. Did we like corn on the cob? We admitted that we had not yet tried that cereal. Of course, our host insisted that we must partake of this American dish. All of these items were delightfully presented by his wife at their retreat which was tastefully concealed up a creek.

Twenty-five miles out of town we settled ourselves in his sanctuary. It was where the family escaped from the sultry heat of down town Baltimore. Nine stone chalet style cabins were secreted in dense woods which offered shade and tranquillity. There was a crystal clear spring, bubbling its cool water which quenched our thirst even as it sparkled in our glass. If one still wilted with the heat there was a superb little swimming pool.

We stayed over night and that really was an experience. The silence was broken by chirping crickets and raucous bull frogs serenading the dusk. Such an unforgettable night where the woodland silence was punctuated by sounds louder than seemed possible, all emanating from these small creatures. Then early morning we were coaxed to life by a vociferous chorus of bird song which penetrated the intense stillness and silence of this sylvan scene. Day-break was sheer magic as the light slowly filtered down through the thick canopy of the trees. When eventually our host drove us back to town late that morning we, two sailors, felt naturalised landlubbers, and were most gratified for his hospitality and his stewardship.

Amongst my many American friendships, outstanding was the bond which I formed with a most remarkable lady. She was the resident doctor at an institution for the inadequate. Isabel would be somewhere over thirty years of age. I was just twenty. We were both unattached, so I found it quite remarkable, that despite our deep affection for each other, our relationship remained platonic.

Isabel was Canadian and proud of her Scottish forebears. Although petite, with her hair swept up in an attractive arrangement on top of her head, she had an air of authority. At the same time, she was elegantly feminine, fragrant, bright and delightfully attractive. I was totally captivated by her warmth and gentle charm.

These were character forming years and I was particularly fortunate to have been befriended by an exemplary and wonderful person. I could not have found a finer tutor or example to admire. She did not lecture but rather lead by example. We attended her church some Sundays simply because she asked if I would like to come along. I was learning the meaning of "true friendship."

I remember one day when we were chatting she seemed to say with a sigh, "Ah, it is... once in a lifetime." At first, I thought it was a throw-away remark, but later upon reflection, I believe she was referring to our relationship. I eagerly looked forward to each weekend to meet her. Probably, I was discovering platonic friendship, from never a heart so true.

Her friend who was often around was even prettier but doubtless aware of her attractions. She was flirting and sitting on my knee with the buttons of her blouse undone, one button too far, and was rebuked by Isabel. Unperturbed, our charming companion then requested that I should wash her hair. This might have developed into an embarrassing game but before further assistance was required, Isabel found a diversion. The friend confided in me that one could be more playful and that Isabel was a bit straight but there was absolutely no question of my ruining the trust and friendship I enjoyed with Isabel. I made that clearly understood.

I would disappear off the ship from the Friday till Monday whilst staying at Isabel's house. We went ten pin bowling with her friends. Occasionally we took in a show and frequently dined out. Isabel had two domestic servants. These girls were members of the institute but had both domestic and culinary skills. Their cooking was excellent and this was despite their learning difficulties. When I praised their apple pie they squirmed with delight and became eager to demonstrate further baking skills. Needless to say, I was very susceptible and encouraged their achievements. Evenings 'at home' were enjoyed playing cards or games with Isabel and her friends.

On one occasion the question was asked whether I would like to dine out, take in a show, go bowling or stop at home. My spontaneous reply was that I would be happier to stop 'at home.' This was taken as a great compliment by Isabel that as hostess, her company and home had priority over outside entertainment. This of course was true and reason enough for my joy being delayed in Baltimore. On the otherhand some crew members became bored with the prolonged stay in port, which proved the benefits of having made such good friends.

I attended the yacht club and enjoyed watching the sleek racing wings speed across the bay. The delightful classic yachts thrilled me as they invariably would in many parts of the world. I have always derived great pleasure from observing sailing craft harnessing the wind. They have an intoxicating effect on a dreamer and certainly, as I watched, I dreamed that one day, I would participate in that sporting life.

The White House, the Pentagon and Washington itself, were sights which we took in our stride, as together we toured the surrounding country. Americans seem to have lots of friends, thus everywhere we travelled, there would be someone to visit, with whom to enjoy a barbecue or picnic alfresco. Good living is a bonus which has to be earned. Dry dock repairs were complete, the ship was fully loaded and we were now about to depart. Gifts were exchanged and there was a great sadness that life had to move on. It is so true that "Farewell goes out sighing."

Isabel gave me a very fine book "A Treasury of the Familiar." It truly was a treasure to gloat over at sea. Poetry and prose were included and it contained many examples of lines which could be located in their original source. Isabel inscribed her present with "To Robert, with Best Wishes for a Happy Voyage, Devotedly, Isabel."

We corresponded frequently and the following Christmas I sent her a card with my thoughts suitably expressed :

Friendship's embers gently fanned,
Soon brighten in the glow,
Of Christmas and New Year
With thoughts of years ago.
How such a depth of feeling,
Can flow from friends unseen.
The spirit of friendship hovers.
How fortunate I've been.
                                        Robert.

It was five years later when we next met. I had swallowed the an-chor and was on vacation from studies. Isabel visited London to attend a Medical Conference. Afterwards she came up to Glasgow to my home and met Mother and Father with whom I was tempo-rarily living. She confided in me that her handbag had been stolen in London and included in the loss was all her credit cards and cheques. Well, I required funds to support my studies and living expenses, since as ex Merchant Navy I did not qualify for any grant. We were now not ex service men but classed as civilians. However, I had saved about one year's salary to pursue my ambi-tions. I was not asked for funds but I gave Isabel seventy-five per cent of my savings and would not accept a refusal. She said that she would repay me in full but I said that it was a gift. I believed of course, that when it was possible, the money would be returned and that she would insist upon my acceptance.

As further expression of our friendship I took her around our be-loved Scotland. The old banger, which I had bought, was for prac-tising as I was learning to drive. I actually failed the driving test because it started to rain, disclosing the fact that I did not have any working windscreen wipers. Overlooking these minor details the car could always disappear in a cloud of blue smoke. Petrol was in short supply but this was eked out by generous additions of paraffin which was more readily available.

I would say that our mode of transport was a thrilling contrast to the limousines to which Isabel was doubtless accustomed. My thrilling mode of transport struggled up some of the mountains and steep inclines, merely managing ten miles per hour. This was accompanied by a dense blue smoke screen blowing out of the exhaust and the occasional hesitating cough. It seemed reasonable when Isabel asked the question, "Will we make it?"

On one occasion, when it rained, the rusty old sunshine roof leaked. This didn't affect our progress but it altered my appearance somewhat! The water gathered in a pool on the underside in the roof lining, until eventually it soaked through and dripped on to my head, my shirt front and finally stained my trousers. Can you imagine how I must have appeared at the reception desk of the hotel? Was my face red? Certainly it was, because the leakage was a red dye and I had to explain that I had not been in an accident and that I was not seriously injured.

As far as Isabel and I were concerned our reaction was to jog along in the old jalopy in happy chorus. We were singing in the rain but it was with the Auld Scottish Songs! We ventured to Loch Lomond, Glen Coe, the Trossachs and those areas I so much enjoy.   Naturally, I derived great pleasure and satisfaction from showing her my native land. This was the least I could do in return for the generous hospitality which I had received previously. Besides, I was feasting on her friendship with keen delight and the pity was that it lasted only two weeks. Then Isabel had to return to Baltimore whilst I resumed my studies.

> *... Had we never lov'd sae kindly,*
> *Had we never lov'd sae blindly,*
> *Never met - or never parted,*
> *We had ne'er been broken-hearted....*
> *Robert Burns.*

An alarming incident happened during the final stage of loading *Loreto.* Large crates were swung on board and carefully stowed to avoid movement. They were pulled across so that they became tightly packed together. A wire hawser was taken round a pulley wheel and then attached to the crate. As the wire was wound on to the drum of a steam winch, it dragged the crate into position. Suddenly, as I watched, the steel pulley wheel snapped out of its block and flew across the dock to strike one of the stevedores on the side of his face. He went down immediately, and in two jerking spasms, he was dead– killed instantly by the blow from the eight inch heavy steel wheel. Work stopped and the workers went home in a state of shock. The following day loading had been completed and quietly we slipped out of the dock with an overwhelming ominous cloud hanging over the ship as we seemed enveloped with a feeling of foreboding .

Before making our way across the Atlantic we had to proceed North to join a convoy. What mariners dread is the deadly fog, and as we entered its dense obscurity, our awareness of foreboding intensified. In mid ocean there is space to sail blind but on a coastal passage, hazards are presented which must be circumvented. Eyes are virtually closed and trust in navigating by dead reckoning is all that remains. The principal threat was Cape Cod which projected from the coast into the Atlantic. It had a fearsome reputation for causing shipwrecks in its past and we were sailing in this blinding fog. Allowances had to be made for wind, current and tide, to be sure that we were not set too far inshore.

It was mid-morning. The fog had thickened and nerves on the bridge were on edge. The cool damp air drifting along with the Labrador current chilled us with shivers as we shrugged our shoulders under our duffel coats. The surface hairs on our coats were sprinkled with droplets of moisture settling out of the fog. Nothing could be seen as we ghosted our way along the coast heaving and rolling in the huge swell. This was the aftermath and all that remained of the recent storm. It was a strange way to be back at sea and to be cloaked in isolation in this grey cloud.

What was that? And that! **We have struck!** We are listing badly and sinking. There are signs of panic on board as some dash to look over the side of the ship but nothing can be seen. The force of impact had thrown some of the crew off balance and they were picking themselves up. There was no doubt we were now stationary, stuck, but swerving round and being pushed over by the swell. Another shuddering and thumping reverberated throughout the ship as we pounded on the rocks. Much more and she could break up!

The captain called the engine room. "Are you all right down below? Are we taking water? Sound the tanks!" The Mate, followed by the bosun was running up forward and started to check the ship's holds to gauge the intake of water. We had already filled half of No.1 hold and it was obvious that there was no way we could move under our own power. We had struck and were firmly stuck on the bottom or lodged on rocks. Even if it were possible, to try to drag her off at this stage it would quickly ensure complete sinking. The situation was grim. The coast station was called on the radio with our emergency message and estimated position reported. So long as we held fast without too much pounding the damage might be controlled.

We were on a falling tide, so provided we did not break up and the weather did not deteriorate, there were the next few hours to assess our predicament, form a plan and try to redress the situation. Soundings were continually taken to measure the ingress of the sea in each of her holds and tanks. The salvage tugs arrived and divers went down to check the damage. Plans were made to discharge our cargo into lighters disposing of as much cargo as possible in the limited time. This work was speedily put in hand and everyone worked feverishly to help lighten the ship. Access to the hull eventually enabled cement blocks to be fixed over the holes and damaged areas of the hull. Work continued throughout the night with all available pumps going flat out. We were very fortunate that the weather did not deteriorate. Eventually the flooding sea was controlled by the blocks and pumps. There was a chance now that if the cargo were removed sufficiently, and with the help of the next tide, she might rise enough for the tugs to drag her off backwards from the rocks.

That was our objective and sometime later, after a great deal of hard work, efforts were rewarded as eventually we limped alongside the salvage tugs as they struggled to guide us into New York. We were in no position to withstand rough seas or high winds. But because weather conditions were inclined to be foggy the winds remained light. Nevertheless it was a nerve- wracking journey as heeled over at an angle we wobbled our way into port. We were thankful when the New York docks hove into view and yet again we found ourselves in dry dock. Some serious patching up was then undertaken.

Looking on the bright side we were in New York. The entertainment was lavish and many free shows were available for servicemen. We had survived so that was something to celebrate. An amazing encounter occurred when I met a girl from almost next door to my home in Glasgow. We went to a Scottish ceilidh together and whirled the night away in reels encouraged by the pipes and 'drams.' This was a grand musical combination which was accompanied by many a delightful whee--oop!

I met several shipmates with whom I had previously sailed. Repeatedly the world was proving to be smaller than I imagined and over the years of travelling countless encounters turned up unexpectedly. Celebrities, cinemas and shows made this another memorable stay. Time just raced by until we learned to our surprise that we had been diverted to sail south for Mobile Alabahma.

We left N.Y. in early December and sailed south in order to have the ship properly repaired before crossing the Atlantic.

As members of her crew, we were having a wonderful time in these ports but the poor ship and her owners were in dire trouble. On her previous voyage she was the only ship to escape destruction in her convoy. The "Scharnhorst" and "Gneisenau" were the attackers and *Loreto* managed to sail into the fog and escaped. Unfortunately the fog and fickle fortune now had their revenge. It was almost disaster and subsequent costs were immense as demonstrated by this further dry docking and repairs. There was also the human cost as the captain was on his way home, probably deposed.

The idea of visiting Mobile, Alabama, on the otherhand, had for me considerable attractions because this was an opportunity to see something of a southern state and, of course, it was winter and the weather south would be kindly, even comfortably warm. When a sailor steps ashore in a strange port he is a conspicuous target for prostitutes, doubtful characters and thieves. Obviously, he has just been paid and money attracts problems. These can usually be controlled by going ashore in company and also by the company which one courts. When first visiting Mobile, I went ashore with Trevor and we soon located a suitable shoreside establishment where music and entertainment beckoned. Everything was going splendidly and there was a honky-tonk type piano from which Trevor could tickle a fair tune. A little group had joined in our singing and we had stimulated a jovial evening. As the night wore on I found myself in conversation with an American guy who suggested that the next drink was on him. He beckoned me over to the bar where he said "Try this rum and coke. It's the favourite drink in these parts." He continued to engage me in conversation until he popped out for a moment to the cloakroom.

At that point the barman said "Look here, sailor, I hope you know what you are doing. You want to look out with that fellow and watch what you are drinking!" I took the hint and went back to join Trevor but already I was feeling off-colour. I demanded that Trevor should accompany me back to the ship and pointed out that the guy pestering me was up to no good. Of course, Trevor was not exactly willing to have the party break up at that stage but eventually he acceded to my demands. We called a taxi and went on our way, although the guy remonstrated with Trevor about interfering with his friend. It seemed obvious now that his intentions had not been honourable.

Next morning I felt exhausted and my right ankle was painful. Examining my right shoe, I could see that the heel was almost pulled off and that the nails had been drawn out and were only just holding it in position. The explanation was soon unravelled. It seemed that I had been slipped a Mickey Finn in that drink by the pest. When Trevor and I negotiated the gangway, I slipped and only the quick action of the night watchman prevented me from falling fifty feet down into the bottom of the dry dock. I was saved by the heel of my shoe which caught between the strips of wood on the gangway but held me dangling upside down over the dock. I marked up another notch on survival.

During our stay in port I inveigled my way into dancing lessons with a dance teacher and she kindly gave me free tuition. Thus, on two afternoons each week, I frolicked on the dance floor gaining confidence with each new step mastered. Christmas and party time was approaching so expertise in these social skills was most opportune. A dance was being held at the largest hotel in town. Sailors have style and that is our expectation but as I walked in with a girl on each arm there was an uproar. The greeting was tumultuous as thundering applause echoed around the hall generated by numerous voices all from my ship. I was truly embarrassed but in a rather delightful way. Throughout the evening, it took stamina to retain the interest of both girls. I succeeded because the girls were sisters and in a competitive way were prepared to share their affections. I responded, but as one can imagine, I had to work doubly hard.

On Christmas Eve the sisters whizzed me round their friends and we toured at least half a dozen houses, having a convivial time and enjoying thoroughly the spirit of the evening. Retiring to their home, I had the problem of avoiding favouritism. I solved this hurdle, by being alternately partial. I believe that there must have been a full moon on that Christmas Eve.

I returned to the ship for Christmas dinner. A truly sumptuous banquet was produced by our cook who had taken endless trouble with the cuisine. As usual on these occasions, not everyone was capable of appreciating his efforts but that meant some of us enjoyed a greater share.

Between parties I tried to ensure that a special night was highlighted with the two sisters. This was, of course, to celebrate my 21st Birthday on the 29th December. Throughout that afternoon and evening I enjoyed "Southern Hospitality" from their various friends. We danced in our stocking soles in several houses with a progressive party pursuing festive fun. Finally, the choreography brought us to the girls' home. My important birthday was emphatically memorable. It included twenty-one hedonistic hours which could not have been sustained in later years. However, I subsequently found that I had a bit of darning to do.

There was scarcely time to recover from these parties and regain an equilibrium to celebrate New Year and that was when I was glad to be "only twenty-one." It took perseverance to do justice to Hogmanay, but I was determined that tradition should not be overshadowed. The New Year was brought in with style! Of course I had the advantage of double helpings!

> .... *When I was one-and-twenty*
> *I heard a wise man say,*
> *"Give crowns and pounds and guineas*
> *But not your heart away;*
> *Give pearls away and rubies*
> *But keep your fancy free."*

But I was one-and-twenty,
No use to talk to me...

A.E.Housman. "A Shropshire Lad."

Was I sorry to leave Mobile? Yes, parting was painful, but such
sweet sorrow! The first league out from land was, at least, physi-
cally glorious even with a broken heart. Gone was the smoke and
noise of the shipyard and the sea air seemed like nectar. I felt as if
I had aged in Mobile! However, after the first day at sea the salt
of life had me condimentally rejuvenated which must be pretty
close to being exalted. Anyway, I was ecstatic, exalted and ex-
hilarated. No doubt it was the sea breezes and proper sleep. Sailing put me right back and up on my toes, with the "good to be
alive" feeling. We called at Tampa in Florida and thence sailed to
Cuba.
Matanzas/Nuevitas in Cuba was where we commenced to load our
cargo of sugar. We were one of the first ships to call during the
restrictions of war. Therefore, extra care was being taken to avoid
a fire in the ship. It was the first occasion on which Radio officers
were called upon to undertake `cargo watches.' Our duties in-
volved observation of workers down in the holds, to prevent
smoking, note fire risks and particularly to watch out for sabotage.
Apart from two small cinemas with Spanish language films and
indifferent restaurants there was nowhere particularly attractive.
However, it was foreign territory, which in itself was different so
that there were interesting walkabouts. Dancing involved rhumba
and similar Spanish movements but so far my gyrations had not
advanced sufficiently to take on those routines.

I purchased a pair of maracas so that when appropriate I could ab-
sorb the Latin tempo. I wondered if riding on the bus had anything to do with the rhumba movements. There was no surface on
the roads which were mere tracks with innumerable pot-holes.
The local bus wobbled at fifteen miles per hour and I thought that
seeing the movements and posteriors of the passengers that they

were making a fair attempt at a rhumba.

There were lots of girls but not the sort to gain our attention. Prostitutes pushing themselves at every turn soon became a pestering nuisance. Purchases which I made were the inevitable sample of local rum and a shark carved from bone. This indigenous species was always highly visible swimming around the ship. As we lay alongside the jetty at least half a dozen fifteen to twenty feet long sharks could be seen swimming beside the ship. They were massive, grey and sinister, slinking to and fro in the sea, just waiting for any form of trash to be thrown overboard from the galley. Whatever gash it might be, they battled furiously and eagerly snapped up any food or waste thrown into the sea. The vicious competition and voracious appetites convinced me that swimming wasn't an option. Nevertheless, the tropical sunshine and clear blue water were enticing. Eventually, I was persuaded that after all we were amphibians. Bathing it appeared was approved, but only at the official swimming pool, just along the beach. This was a protected pool! Stout metal wire mesh netting had been fixed into the seabed and up to the surface creating a stout protective surrounding screen. In the middle of the pool a floating raft was anchored where one could rest and enjoy sun-worshipping. I was persuaded that this was a safe enclosure for a swim. My fellow radio officer was convincing and very keen that I should accompany him. We both entered the pool and our objective was to swim out to the raft. We both swam out to the platform and commented on the exhilarating experience. The water was sparkling clear and delightfully warm. Lying in the sun on the anchored raft was idyllic. Then my gaze wandered towards the sea. Good Lord! Look at that! There it was - a great gaping hole about twenty feet wide in the netting. Obviously this was shark damage and any shark which had gained entry would not find its way back out again. The wired pool would function like a bottle neck fish trap and there would be no escape. Any shark in the pool would be trapped and must now be very hungry.

I was still haunted by visions of those monsters swimming along-side the ship and how quickly and ferociously they swallowed. Who was going to risk swimming back? Who was mad enough to dive back into the shark infested pool? It was obvious after half an hour's inspection of the water that my trembling companion was not going to be the first. It took some time to realise that there was no alternative but to have a go! I am not a swimmer by any standards but I got ashore pretty dammed quick! I called to my friend but he was rigid. There was no way he was going to be shark bait. I was patient and reassuring but it was at least an hour before he weakened in his resolve to live. He then dived in and creating a fantastic bow wave, he finally made it.

The explanation which we later gathered was that the pool had been out of commission for years, ever since ships had ceased to call. It was confirmed that if a shark had ventured into the pool we would not have been able to explain the circumstances. The dreaded look of that gaping hole in the wire, inviting those sharks to enter, still haunts me. Diving back into that pool was one of my bravest acts. We were petrified and justly imagined that we were in the greatest danger. We survived, but almost qualified for another survival notch!

When we left Cuba we sailed across the delightful Gulf of Mexico gently heaving and rolling in dreamlike conditions. Beautiful blue tropical sea with a fresh breeze and the blazing sun made the experience idyllic. These waters were a tropical paradise.

> ...."Oh sweet it was in Aves, to hear the landward breeze,
> A swing with good tobacco, in a net between the trees.
> With a negro lass to fan you, while you listen to the roar.
> Of the breakers on the reef outside that never touch
> the shore."...

> "The Old Buccaneer." Charles Kingsley.

Leaving the beautiful islands and Bahamas we soon encountered the Sargasso Sea. There are stories of sailing ships being trapped in this area of thick sea weed. The weed reputedly was so dense that a ship could be held fast for weeks, unable in the light winds, to break free. The crew inevitably would go mad with thirst and then eventually die of starvation. Such beliefs are now dispelled because although the weed is very thick in places, it tends to be in patches. The weed, which collects in vast quantities, floats on the surface, where it gathers in a powerful eddy in the sea. Portuguese sailors named the weed, because of the appearance of air-bladder floats resembling a small grape, they know as sarga. There is estimated to be some ten million tons of the weed in the area. When some is tipped out on to the deck, all sorts of small crabs, snails and tiny fish tumble out. Shells of tiny worms are attached to the fronds of the weed. All of the shells spiral in the same direction. A fascinating exercise in exploration is offered to the curious. It is quite remarkable ploughing through the weed and noticing how it strings out in long lines with the current.

An interesting fact emerges considering that the area of weed is the haunt and breeding place of eels. Their offspring, the elvers, swim in the Gulf Stream across to Europe. This demonstrates another wonderful example of natural migration. At least, we can be thankful that the warm air blowing over this sea at the start of the the Gulf Stream is held responsible for the warmer weather of Europe.

It would be remiss at this point not to mention the **Bermuda Triangle** through which we had to sail. We ventured into that area where the "Triangle Mystery" still baffles. This is the mystery zone where dozens of planes, thousands of men and countless ships have disappeared without trace. It is an area plagued over the years with disasters and so far no suitable explanations have been found. This has been happening for at least 300 years. Apart from losses which have been the result of war, more losses have occurred in this area than anywhere else in the Atlantic.

Occasionally, manless ships have been found with no trace of their crew. There was "La Dahama" and the "Marie Celeste" found abandoned with no sign of any crew and no explanation. There was the nuclear submarine that disappeared in 1968 and the aeroplanes "Star Tiger" and "Star Ariel" in 1948 which at different times simply vanished. Various theories have been formulated from statistically insignificant to magnetic field anomalies. It is known that there are only two places on the globe where the compass points to true north. One is in the "Bermuda Triangle" and the other is the "Devil's Sea." Normally the compass points to magnetic North. Some confusion has been known to be associated with loss of direction but arguments are not strong enough to fully explain these mysteries. Some offer the thought that there is a black hole in the vicinity through which many might have vanished. There are as many explanations as there are mysteries but I took comfort in the thought that many more have passed through the triangle than have ever disappeared.

We then proceeded in good style across the Atlantic as the centre of attraction. We were, on that occasion, the Commodore's ship, front row, middle of the convoy. We had the necessary accommodation for his small elite staff. The only difference was that our signalling and operations on the bridge, had to be extra slick and an overall polished performance was expected.

The galley boy left Cuba feeling he was a hero. He certainly had admirers and many that envied his conquests ashore. He vividly described his love scenes to a captive audience. After the first week at sea he was seeking medical attention for his problems. Ere long, he had the full list of venereal diseases in the doctor's guide book. A dreadful running sore on the side of his face was alone sufficient to have him isolated in separate accommodation. He was ostracised with his own mug and plates. He no longer had any friends and was abhorred as unclean. The deposed hero deteriorated rapidly until he became a pathetic sight. A salutary lesson was demonstrated for anyone contemplating the pleasures of the docks.

Nearing the UK. we were made aware of Wulf pack threats which were leaked to the Commodore, from his intelligence sources, he made the decision to have the convoy alter course to avert disaster. One of his staff issued the order but unfortunately he sent the message by Morse and when interpreted from that code book, it demanded different actions from the flag signal book. The convoy instead of all turning in one direction, each ship dashed independently to its final destination. All of our ships were considered most fortunate to have escaped dire consequences. An enquiry was held ashore and I was glad not to be involved, but all was well, since everyone featured in the great escape.

We docked in Liverpool and could reflect upon the marvellous voyage which we had just enjoyed and the sincere friendships forged. The only shipmate with whom I still have any contact, sailed with me on the *mv.Loreto.* We regularly keep in touch and it is delightful when in nostalgic mood to fondly reminisce on our voyage together on the *mv. Loreto* This was the voyage wherein the knot of life tied in my youth was untied.

——oOo——

8

NORTH ABOUT

I enjoyed my leave and was recalled to London to join a large passenger ship. My appointment anticipated my being in charge of the public address system and the various speakers and communications throughout the ship. Possibly, I would be enrolled on a course to brush up on specialised skills. In order to enhance my chances of this appointment I said that during my leave, I had achieved an extra qualification and gained my senior Post Master General Certificate. That scuppered the appointment immediately. I was now Chief Radio Officer potential. I was not pleased at being directed instead to take charge of the coastal vessel the *SS.META* 2,000Grt. although this was merely a temporary posting.

I sailed in her up the East coast in the company of the *ss.Samcebu,* which as you may remember, was the Liberty ship on which I sailed on her maiden voyage. Again we called into Methil where I met a fellow Sparks from *mv.Loreto.* As further proof of a shrinking world, in Blyth I was able to renew acquaintance with the crew of the little Estonian ship, *ss.Sulev.* Altogether, it was an interesting trip voyaging round the North of Scotland, then South through the Western Isles to Liverpool whilst encountering seafaring friends along the way.

9

V.E. DAY

The spirit of adventure and surprise haunts us in this life and upon arrival in Liverpool, my instructions were to proceed to Bombay, as passenger on board the *ss. MOOLTAN.* It is strange to contemplate the degree of independence which we were afforded and was expected in our operations. I had nobody to consult about my travelling plans. I had no companions en route and every ship and crew were complete strangers. It was left to one's own initiative to forge friendships at each stage. All of this, I suppose was taken in my stride and I regarded each change as another exciting challenge. I proceeded up to Greenock where I boarded the *Mooltan* to travel to Bombay as a Passenger(1st.Class). As we sailed for the Far East it seemed that the end of the war in Europe was imminent. Likewise it appeared that I was heading into the only war area now remaining which of course was out East.

... Ship me somewhere East of Suez
where the best is like the worst
where there aint no ten commandments
and a man can raise a thirst. ...
                              R. Kipling.

V.E. DAY was spent on board the ss.*MOOLTAN* and celebrated with wine which was the only alcoholic beverage available. However, gin was provided by the Captain who ordered drinks to be served to officers on the lower bridge and this was followed by the celebratory V.E.Day dinner served in the saloon.

We were rigged in our full whites with temperatures in the nineties as slowly we melted into the warmth and constrictions of the Suez Canal. The captain was an excellent host and had a fund of stories with which he regaled us. A magician then performed, intending to be mystical, but the misty alcoholic haze he was expected to penetrate resulted in his being perceived as a comedian. It followed that before very long everyone joined in a sing-song and celebrations were well underway. As a tug was passing the Suez Canal signal station, it blew its whistle sounding victory "V`s" and sending up rockets. That was sufficient for every ship to join in the jamboree until vessels for miles around had their sirens sounding "··· — ··· — ··· —", V's. I even heard a train somewhere ashore blasting off with its whistle. This cacophony went on for several hours to the accompaniment of our medley of popping corks.

I have remarked before, that invariably someone, probably a lady, takes centre stage on every passenger ship. Ours was no exception. This amazing nymphomaniac distinguished herself by always having three or four hopeful male suitors drinking at her table. She behaved like the Siren in the Odyssey who enticed seamen to their doom. Undoubtedly, she was successful, as her victims were overcome by alcohol or amour depending upon her preference. The outcome was obvious early in the afternoon as her first victor surfaced from amongst her suitors. Then later he seemed to disappear probably exhausted. Before sundown she again had an entourage of fresh combatants ready and willing to be captivated. What amazed everyone was that she always had several suitors keenly seeking her attention. Several of them visibly wilted under her alcoholic spell and simply faded away. Our lady called the shots and as she manipulated the chosen few those she discarded were seductively encouraged to drown. She,herself, never wavered yet she seemed to be drinking her share. We amused ourselves by gambling to pick the daily winner who might make it to the boudoir. At least that provided us with an excuse to closely scrutinise these machinations.

One brilliant sunny afternoon we were sailing along enjoying the soft, sea breeze. Conditions were blissful, and lazing in the sun, the troops were sprawled out cooling themselves on the deck. In the forward holds, conditions were crowded, but they were taking turns to come up for air and have a spell on deck. They lay in the sun looking up to catch the odd glimpse of this entrancing creature. She was strolling to and fro on the boat deck occasionally coming and going out of sight. Of course, she had the entourage jostling for a position beside her. The jealousy of the troops down below, could be felt and overheard in their mutterings as they sensed the situation with those privileged officers aloft there on the boat deck. Eventually, all the eager admiring faces, looking up from down there, became too much for her ladyship. They were a challenge and had to be captivated by her femininity. She poised at the top of the stairs leading down from the boat deck. Her knee length flimsy summer dress wafted gently in the breeze. Instantly, there was a hushed, total silence. The troops fell spellbound in expectation. The eyes and faces of those below concentrated and gazed upwards in anticipation of their temptress.

The breeze wafted a tease more, so she leaned back slightly to feign conversation with the chap behind. This was too much for the troops. They could refrain no longer from whistling their approval as they obviously were clamouring for more. She took one step further down the stairs and her dress, catching a little breeze, lifted sufficiently to bring tumultuous cheers from all the troops. Our ladyship hesitated, if those cheers meant approval, then a brief moment positioned for admiration, was her natural inclination. She then continued her descent of the stairs and to all those fine fellows down there, she called out "Did you like that?" There was uproar! There was cheering, laughter, badinage. It was uproarious fun and even the *ss.Mooltan* vibrated in the excitement. Again her ladyship was undoubtedly the winner and this time it was practically over the entire ship's company.

Sailing through a canal is a fascinating experience. Each canal is different but the thrill of scenes continually changing along the banks is what generates a passenger's interest. The Suez Canal weaving through the desert is unique. It has no locks since the Mediterranean and the Red Sea are at the same level. Ferdinand de Lesseps organised the construction of the canal in 1869. It is 171 km (106 miles) long. Its magnificent inauguration was graced by a host of European Princes and the Empress Eugene. Guiseppe Verdi composed "Aida" for the occasion and it was performed at the Cairo Opera Theatre.

The town of Suez is at the Southern entrance and Port Said is at the Mediterranean end. Ships take fifteen hours to traverse its length which includes the Little and the Great Bitter Lakes which are all part of the canal system. We halted at Port Said before passing through and of course were entertained by numerous bum boats. (The origin of "bum-boat" is probably from scavenging boats removing filth from ships in the Thames or silt from the bottom of the river in the seventeenth century). These bum-boat traders, as of old, carried goods to sell to ships in the harbour. The sales' pressure exerted on the troops and passengers was fascinating.

Observing the antics of men climbing up ropes to board ship, squabbling between themselves to achieve a customer's attention, and all the bargaining ploys were priceless amusement. Provided one is not involved, this entertainment can be a pleasant form of relaxation. Discerning passengers would reserve their accommodation as Port-Out, Starboard-Home through the Canal and Red Sea and this was known as travelling "POSH." This was the favoured booking when voyaging out East with the `P.& O.' Shipping Line and the origin of the term. It provided fresher air conditions and reduced the rigours of the Red Sea and sun but only slight reduction to sales' pressures.

Next, we entered the Indian Ocean and this provided us with

SS.MOOLTAN built 1923 for P.&O Shipping Co. 21,000 Grt. 15 knts. Passenger/Troopship. Converted to Armed Merchant Cruiser. I sailed 1/5/45 London to Bombay with V.E.Day en route.

131

fresher sailing but we were wary of lurking Japanese submarines so we did not linger. It was full speed ahead until Bombay appeared on the horizon.

10

INDIAN COAST

Arriving in Bombay, the first obstacle was to retrieve my luggage. I had watched the troops helping to 'stow' passenger's gear and I was not amused. Instead of carrying cases, they simply tipped them down steps and laughed at the antics of each package, as it tumbled on its way to the bottom of the hold. It was hardly surprising that my large suitcase was missing. It took several days running about various offices and departments before it was finally located. Fortunately, in true nautical fashion, it had been roped on the outside. The lock was now broken, the sides were split open and having removed the contents, it was fit only to be jettisoned. One chap with a metal chest, found it had been reshaped. When the troops declare war, avoid the target area at all costs.

Initial accommodation in Bombay was on board a passenger ship in Bombay, *ss.TALMA.* Seafarers usually prefer to be housed on a ship rather than a hotel, hoping to escape the heat of these parts. The freshness of a sea breeze was, again, most welcome.

Another quick hop and I found myself appointed as 1st Radio Officer of the **SS.BINFIELD,** of the British India Steam Navigation Company.(B.I.S.N.C.). I had the backing of my second and third R/O's. The third R/O, in particular, was a jazz fiend and with his gramophone we were enlivened by his jovial jam sessions. The British India Steam Navigation Company was the major British shipping company in eastern waters. There were over one hundred ships in the company although about half were lost in World

War Two. Those serving on ships between India and Britain were referred to as being on the 'Home Line' whilst 'Coast Men' were those on the Indian coastal trade. They would be stationed in Bombay, Calcutta, Singapore or Mombassa. Their families would reside in these ports for the spell of two and a half years before returning to the UK. for five months home leave. It was not surprising that 'Coast' men could consume vast quantities of gin after sunset and were regarded as an elite group of sahibs. Captains were known as 'Commanders' in order to avoid any confusion of rank with army captains who were frequently carried as passengers.

The works of Kipling were as relevant to them as those of Robert Burns are to a Scot. The influence of the Raj and the accepted supremacy of the 'Whites' was the culture instilled in me as I soaked up the flavour of India from the B.I. As a British officer I had a "Boy" to look after me. He was in his fifties but on the request of "Gusl saf karo!"(bath clean do) my afternoon bath would be run. Every request was undertaken by an enthusiastic response to please. Servitude seemed to be regarded as a privilege and every request was always performed with a smile. Presumably, the higher the rank of those whom they served the greater was their kudos. We in turn had to respect their admiration and strove to be worthy of their compliance. I also adopted the habit of "Tiffin" as afternoon tea was called. Again this was courteously served with smiles and cultural compatability exuded in every action. The monsoon broke and torrential rain provided me with another encounter with nature. To witness snow, may be remarkable, and likewise it was to experience the onslaught of this unrelenting deluge. The downpour exceeded anything I had imagined and was incessant for weeks at a time. There was some flooding, but nothing serious in the vicinity of Bombay. The decks were of course shrunken, because of the strong the sun. Thus inevitably, deckhead leaks appeared and some required urgent attention. It was amazing how quickly mould appeared, particularly on leather materials. The mould grew profusely and could actually be peeled off. Doeskin uniform trousers and jacket, or serge suiting garments were mostly affected. It was of course the combination of warmth and damp which promoted the fungi and the organic materials supplied the food.

Splitter, splatter, walloping raindrops thumping on the leaking decks. Then they drip through, never ceasing, what a blinking life, by heck! Well, the answer was not to sit around bemoaning the incessant rain but to set to and get cracking. We stripped the wireless room and repainted everything stationary. Then we replaced the wires and gear, finishing off the brass work with any remaining elbow grease. We then engineered with devilish satisfaction invitations to other ships' radio officers to come on board for a chota peg (a small nip). Just by chance they would notice our radio room where instruments sparkled, brass and copper gleamed, everything ship shape and Bristol fashion. They were green with envy. It had proved worth the effort!

One evening the Chitty Wallah (errand boy) appeared with a note for me from the Marconi Office. I had to report next morning to join another ship. That was typical sod's law! Work hard for days, making everything spick and span, only to find oneself being moved. This was the second occasion that it had happened to me so a mental note was made. If wanting to move, refurbish! The remainder of that evening was spent packing, ready for the transfer.

———oOo———

11

PILGRIMS TO MECCA

I had heard incredible tales about pilgrim ships on the Coast. They were packed even tighter than the overcrowded trains or buses seen in Bombay. Such ships were primitive in the extreme. Fetid, intensive, living conditions in the sweat and heat, meant appalling losses amongst those on board. The Red Sea ports of call were suffocatingly hot and not suited to the settlement of "Whites" hence it was not surprising that everyone steered well clear to avoid such a posting.

At the Marconi office I learned that I had to join the *SS. KHOSROU* of the MOGUL line of India. She was 4000 Grt. and at anchor out in Bombay Bay. I had to obtain the services of a boatman to ferry me and my gear out to the ship.

It was obvious, wasn't it? This was the nearest thing to a "pier head jump"! Once on board it would be difficult to make the return trip ashore. This scenario prompted me to ask a few more questions. These confirmed my suspicions that I was about to learn some first hand experience of the "Pilgrim Trade." Actually, the thought of the deprivations, the incredible hardships and the opportunity to experience such an adventure of primitive proportions seemed a real challenge. Short of paddling up the Amazon in a canoe there was no jungle adventure for a sailor. It could not be as terrible as it had been portrayed. On the contrary, in reality it was nautical despondency at the lowest point on the deprivation scale.

I climbed on board and I could sense immediately that this ship

136

was remarkably different. I was starting on an adventure which would be an unrivalled experience. I was greeted with deference and addressed as "EK Burra Marconi Sahib." (No.1 Big Chief Marconi Sir). I had a `Boy` at my beck an call and the support of my second radio officer who was also a Scot. It is amazing how many exported Scots could be found throughout the world in the most remarkable and remote places. I regarded this as a reflection of our pioneering spirit and considered that I was about to commence the adventure of a lifetime.

The first night on board I did not sleep too well as I had developed an irritating itch which left me with numerous red pimples. I suspected that I was an early victim of a tropical disease which had already captured me unawares and was starting to develop. The following night however, the diagnosis of the condition was obvious. The problem was starving bed bugs welcoming their fresh food supply. The mattress or straw palliasse otherwise described as the "donkey's breakfast" was heaving with these little brown creatures which have a characteristic smell when squeezed. This is one of the smells of India which I can still vividly recall. I changed the mattress and disinfected the bunk hoping for a good night`s sleep, but a few more lessons had to be learned. Battles can be won but there was a constant insect war to be waged aboard the Mogul Line ships.

Afternoon tea was served with the obligatory slice of warm buttered toast. This was pleasant only after a few wrinkles were learned. The tea was better taken without sugar. I discovered the tea leaves which seemed to float on the surface of the cup turned out to be ants and not all of them were dead. The sugar was alive with ants and when added to the tea the ants floated out on top. These could be spooned off the surface but this was tedious and not entirely successful. The most obvious solution was to avoid adding sugar. Ants could of course be consumed as a source of protein but as they were likely to be present in other foods I avoided those spoiling my cup of tea. Brown ants were everywhere and while lying on my bunk they would sometimes provide an interesting diversion from heat exhaustion. They would run in a long line, weaving across the white painted wooden panels of the bulkhead. Carrying food particles, they scurried to and fro in never ending activity. It was always worth checking on their food source, as I would likely be their supplier. Ants were particularly fond of sweet products. Something like Turkish delight would disappear in a trice. It postponed destruction if the temptation was suspended on a piece of string dangling from the deckhead (ceiling). Even so demolition might only be delayed by a day, depending of course, upon the quantity involved. But it was fascinating, observing the way they unerringly located the food and organised a workforce to transport it back to their base camp. If I drew a finger across the line of travelling ants, killing a few in the process, there was panic! Turmoil ensued, with some ants carting away their dead, some reorganising a new line of workers, until eventually full production was resumed. Nothing could stop their plundering. Brown ants will eat everything resembling food. Once demolition is started they will not be diverted until their task is completed. They both smell and taste horrible.

If I introduced black ants to these brown ants then it was a full scale war. Amazing battles could be watched until the red ants, who were in the majority, overwhelmed the intruders. Black ants are slender, nimble and sprightly and less likely to take over chunks of food or become ensconced in the jam. They tend not to spoil the source of food and seem to prefer dead cockroaches.

That was the friendly aspect of one's insect or crustacean companions, but there was the horrible, creepy-crawly, scavengers, that would happily eat one alive! These were the giant repugnant cockroaches (cockroach Americana). Known locally as Bombay canaries, they had a four to five inch body, with long weaving antennae projecting from a repulsive head and powerful jaws. I detested those long creepy feelers and as the cockroaches wafted them about I squirmed and recoiled as the shudders ran through me. Were I to bash a scurrying cockroach, killing it with my shoe, the result was revolting. A large yellow mass of pus would ooze out of the body and make cleaning up the floor nauseatingly difficult.

Consider the night when I was sleeping soundly, until I became aware of something on my pillow. I could hear and feel the cockroach fiddling about near my ear, possibly seeking the way in. I awoke alert and twitching nervously as I brushed it away with a quick swipe of my hand. Recoiling from my attacker and its abhorrent long antennae, I did not see where it fell.

Once more during that night, I had to defend myself as the repugnant creature returned or perhaps it was another of its fraternity. However, a tired radio operator needs his sleep, so I was soon deep in slumbers once more. Then I became just aware, that I was jerking my foot a couple of times but sleep made this reaction a shadowy, dreamy sensation. Until, wow! I awoke with a jump and pulled up my foot. There hanging on to my big toe, with its mandibles firmly embedded, was a detestable giant cockroach. Apparently, it had been eating the hard skin on the base of my big toe, until it took that last bite into the quick when it had drawn blood. The pain was sufficient to jerk me wide awake. There was an area of skin missing around the hole it had eaten from my toe. It was horrible! This time, it was hunt the cockroach and I took my revenge, because I was well prepared to clean up the mess or consequences! That is still not as disgusting as what might be happening, if one ventures up to the fo'c's'tle. This is up forward in the bow of the ship where the Lascars sleep.   One could find a giant cockroach perched on the lip of a crew member, picking out the food from between his teeth as it feasted. It is not strange, therefore, that I was prepared to lose some sleep rather than have my **teeth cleaned!**
On the subject of insects, the dangerous ones were the mosquitoes. When being menaced by them I slept with a mosquito net over my bunk as this was essential for protection. It was most

SS.KHOSROU.built 1924. 4,043 Grt. Mogul Line Bombay. Pilgrim Ship,Jeddah on Hajj.
Ek Number Burra Marconi Saab. July 1945 to April 1946.

uncomfortable as it restricted air flow. In hot sultry humid conditions, breathing was a laboured exercise in survival. The net was tolerated only because of the humming buzzing sounds of the hovering insects flying around the outside of the net trying to find their way through for a biting attack. It sounded rather like bombers droning overhead but if securely fastened the net protected me. However, I must have been bitten during the day when I was perambulating about. I succumbed to malaria and it is not a pleasant experience, especially in the conditions in which I had to endure and recover from this disease. When I say recover, that was from that particular initiation of the problem because recurring outbreaks plagued me from that day.

I have not mentioned the mundane common cockroaches because they were a fact of life and present in all ships. Infestation varied only in degree and what was important was the number and size of the particles which found their way into cooked food. Minute sections were acceptable but whole cockroaches and large body parts could affect my appetite. Semolina was never a favourite because bodies of insects or maggots were too apparent.

Never look at food being prepared and keep well clear of the galley. On one ship, when on the midnight to four am watch, I had a penchant for a hot thick slice of buttered toast well spread with marmalade. I would pop down to the galley to make this delicacy. When the light was switched on I was astounded at the brown coloured walls. The colour started to open up and reveal white bulkheads which had been completely covered with brown cockroaches. I watched with amazement as thousands of these creatures spread out to disappear into crevices and cracks to hide from the light. It didn't put me off my toast though I recognised an appalling infestation. As a general rule it is unwise to venture near the galley if you wish to enjoy food. Where possible I avoided seeing the preparation of food particularly with native curries which often incur doubtful practices best kept out of view. The insect population on board the *ss. KHOSROU* could match anything afloat but so long as they were not too obvious in the food I was not unduly concerned.

One day I saw the Goanese steward taking `chota hazree'(early morning tea) to the captain. The 'Boy' wore a white patrol jacket buttoned up to the neck and overall our services appeared immaculate. He delivered the cup of tea on its saucer with a slice of delectable toast. Then he went and stood outside the Chief Engineer`s cabin for a moment whilst he pulled out a slice of toast from his jacket pocket, put it on the plate, and proceeded to enter the cabin. What was even more amazing was the fact that he used his left hand. The left hand should never be used when eating food or touching another person. The religious taboo centres on the fact that it is only the left hand which is used for personal hygiene and cleansing purposes.

The Mogul Line of India had seven passenger cargo ships. Each one was named after a Mogul Emperor. Except for the captain, chief engineer and chief radio officer the crew was Indian. These ships plied the Indian coast and traded West, as far as the Mediterranean, with all ports en route. The design of each ship was similar to the **Khosrou** with accommodation arranged particularly suited to pilgrim passengers. Since the objective was economy for the passengers and profit for the ship owner, it seemed the more passengers transported the better. Thus at 4,ooo tons Grt. we carried about as many passengers as the "Queen Mary" of 81,000 tons. We took 1500 per trip which was the capacity for the "Queen Mary," but of course when acting as a troop carrier her numbers were greatly increased.

Sometimes we appeared to have exceeded our passenger capacity but that might imply some fiddling by the agents or that some of the visitors remained on board when saying goodbyes. Both deviants did happen. Certainly it caused one to reflect upon sardines and to consider when was the ship comfortably full? I felt that we did not have a vestige of space left for one single extra passenger.

Our arrangements anticipated that most passengers would sleep on deck. Thus, practically every five feet by two feet of deck space was accommodation for one person. We had two flat decks running from the bow to the stern. Imagine each deck 400ft long and 50 ft wide crammed with sleeping bodies. It was an amazing spectacle. Even more remarkable, was the congestion when all were standing up and trying to move around. It makes understatements of mass or multitude. I had to survive in the midst of the congestion coupled with intense heat and high humidity. It is probably unimaginable to describe the extreme fatigue and debilitation one suffered as the environment sapped feelings of life beyond mere existence.

Before the start of the Pilgrim Trade, we left Bombay with a few hundred passengers as our normal passenger and cargo handling business. Our first port of call was hot steamy Aden. Coming from India this would be descriptive but if escaping from the incredibly hot stifling Red Sea area, then Aden is somewhat cooler. We normally anchored in the bay, off steamer point. Looking towards the shore, I could well understand the Scottish bagpipe tune "The Barren Rocks of Aden." This is a precise description since Aden is built on the site of past volcanic activity. It looked dry and crumbly, but its main attraction was the port's convenient location on the major sea route between India and Europe. In 1839 the acquisition of Aden by Britain enabled the strategic control of shipping and the British ruled their South Arabian Protectorate from Aden. The army was ensconced there throughout the war.

Aden was our regular port of call. We invariably spent two days anchored in the bay, exchanging passengers and cargo. Ashore there was little to see and to venture to Crater or further inland was not regarded as entirely safe, since at that time the situation was volatile and relations disturbed. Needless to say, curiosity eventually persuaded me to take a look at the ancient town of Crater on a subsequent call. Meantime a walk ashore was pleasant exercise and a relief from our moderately crowded ship. I do also recall that the ice cream available was something about which we would fantasise. Combating the heat, ice cream routinely slipped down as a wonderful relief from our perpetual diet of hot curries. It also says a lot about the state of our existence and deprivations, if a simple ice cream could give such a spiritual lift.

Our next port of call was Suez which was founded in 15th Century as a pilgrims' stop over, between Cairo and Mecca. We actually berthed at Port Tewfik Island, which is an outlying part of the town, situated on a short causeway at the southern entrance to the canal and it is a splendid spot from which to view the ships as they appear occasionally to move magically through the desert. The water in the canal frequently cannot be seen at a distance because of the height of the canal sides and this results in a ship appearing to move mysteriously through the desert.

Suez itself is eighty-five miles from Cairo and there is a useful rail link across wadi-scoured desert between the towns. In order to look around Suez the second Sparks and I hired bicycles and rode the two miles from Port Tewfik into the town. We were amused with the brown paper wrappings still covering the frames of the bicycles. The ride was a pleasant relaxation and we found a more intimate appreciation of the differences between the wealthier sub-urban type dwellings in tree lined Port Tewfik, as opposed to the squalid town areas of Suez.

In the afternoon, one could enjoy a cool drink in the open air cinema. The seats and tables were on an earth floor, about which there was a low surrounding wall, preventing passers-by from seeing a free cinema show. The film was not shown until evening. When the sun went down and darkness took over then the film started up. It was rather pleasant sitting out in the open air under a canopy of stars with a whitened wall functioning as the screen.

The Arab operator did not always follow the reel sequence, since No.4 might be shown before reel No.3. The fact that the cowboy is shot dead on the street but then is later seen in the bar drinking, can thus be explained. These minor upsets provided amusing interludes which could only be found in such strange haunts.

Returning to Bombay, we sailed with our complement of passengers. We had a Nawab dressed in exotic gilded attire together with his courtiers. Also there was a Turkish princess and a Marquis, rather an elite group contrasting sharply with our future complement of pilgrims. In Bombay, the ship was chipped and painted to reinstate her to peace time colours. The hull colour was changed to black with a wide white band running round the ship. The superstructure became a dazzling white and the black funnel now had two white bands enclosing a red band in between. The transformation was dramatic considering the overall, drab war time grey, previously experienced.

Preparation was also under way for the forthcoming pilgrims. Suitable pens were fitted to hold sheep, goats and poultry. We did not have refrigeration to supply meat for the Pilgrims, hence the need for live animals which would be ritually slaughtered as required. Latrines were installed on deck, water stand pipes were mounted for ablutions and down below the holds were painted white throughout in readiness for the great throng.

Meantime I went ashore and to my surprise the Dhobi Wallah still held some of my gear which I had been unable to collect before sailing. It was only shorts and several shirts but a welcomed insight into the ways of the Dhobi Wallah.(laundry man). He had kept them for me although I wasn't exactly an old customer. I presume he retained gear for some months but with no tickets or identification it was an amazing system. I had already learned that the local shirts were of a fabric designed to be thrashed against the stones and capable of surviving the pummelling which the dhobi wallah meted out. Thick strong cotton whites came back in pristine condition whereas western wear would be in tatters.

Exhilaration and delight followed when a nine-page letter from my Doctor friend and other American heart throbs arrived with my correspondence. Mail from home and friends was wonderful cheer when remotely stationed out East. The cinema in Bombay was air conditioned and surprisingly it felt cold. Likewise there was the comforting onslaught of delightfully warm air when we escaped outside again to the heat of town.

Leaving Bombay the next stop was Karachi to embark our Pilgrim Passengers. The refurbished ship was now fully equipped to even include shops on deck for the sale of drinks and sundries. Beehive type tandoori ovens had been installed on deck so that the baker could turn out the thousands of chapatti which would be required. Just before we became overwhelmed with our human cargo we slipped ashore to Karachi town for a brief respite and enjoyed a cycle ride about its wide clean streets. The Merchant Navy Club was a really superb building erected in 1944 as a tribute and token of respect for the war time efforts of the gallant men of the Merchant Navy- a truly admirable monument, with practical overtones, which we fully appreciated.

Once more I was fascinated by local sailing craft. On this occasion it was the outrigger canoes with the crew nimbly perched high out on his pole. The skill of the balancing act which he performed sliding out or inboard in sympathy with the wind was quite remarkable. This was all the more so because I was familiar with the tenderness of these dugout canoes. We had one at home and as my brother and I sailed it under the main road bridge we stopped all the traffic overhead. A great crowd gathered looking down from the bridge to the river below, as two young boys seeking adventure, gallantly sailed by with their lateen sail hoisted. Mother saw the crowd and curiously became an observer. When she saw it was her boys on the river below, dangerously close to being drowned, her concern and consternation fortunately dispelled any room for maternal wrath. Recollecting this episode, I immediately wrote home telling brother Jim that we would have to fit an outrigger to our canoe to improve our performance and others' amazement.

My companion, the Second Radio Officer, was highly amused with the camel which pulled a four- wheeled pneumatic tyred cart. The swinging gait of the camel with its weaving footwork and flopping lower lip, admittedly, was a strange sight to western eyes. John certainly found it really hilarious and had to be restrained from reacting with equally ludicrous laughter.

There was certainly nothing to laugh about as we watched the multitude of pilgrims congregating on the quay, before starting to mount our gangway. The procession winding its way on board was in perpetual motion. Even the next day when the ship was absolutely crammed full pilgrims were still mounting the gangway and squeezing on board. Until, at long last, we set off overfilled with our complement of Pilgrims for Mecca.

The Hajj is the pilgrimage to the holy city of Mecca. It is a holy command to Muslims to make the pilgrimage at least once during their life. Thus for many, it takes a lifetime of saving to be able to make this journey. In the year of 1945, when I was involved, conditions were still at a primitive level. 100,000 pilgrims might proceed on the Hajj, coming throughout the world from every direction. Caravans could take months making their way from Egypt across the Sinai desert. Some of our passengers would travel right across India, perhaps spending weeks on the way, with a further five to ten weeks from Bombay to complete the journey. Nowadays, something in excess of two million make this pilgrimage. Air travel, liners, and modern transport, make the journey achievable within two or three weeks.

There was no harbour at Jeddah, the Red Sea port of disembarkation for Mecca. Pilgrims were ferried ashore in small sailing boats and when landed at Jeddah all they would find would be a few dusty primitive houses. These slanted over precariously, from opposite sides of a narrow passage, so that they almost touched at the top. In fact, as they leant over towards the opposite houses, they were occasionally kept apart by pieces of wood jammed between the upper opposing windows. There was nothing else, except for a long desert track. Along this dusty path the pilgrims would have to walk the fifty miles to Mecca.

Today, there is the town of Jeddah with its air-conditioned hotels, the airport, houses and shops. The oil boom has enabled modernisation to mushroom up from the desert. This phenomenal growth can be witnessed elsewhere in these Eastern parts. Bahrain has similarly sprung up from the desert to achieve the status of a modern town and strangely, if the oil disappeared, then the sand would soon reclaim its previous control and the desert again would rule overall.

Mohammed made a last journey to Mecca before he died and the pilgrims follow in his footsteps according to his command: "Oh People, God commands you to make this Pilgrimage to this House so that he may reward you with Paradise." Thus the **Hajj** is one of the **Five Pillars of Islam.**

FIVE PILLARS OF ISLAM.

SHAHADA	**Confession of FAITH.**
SALAH	**PRAYER five times daily.**
ZAKAH	**ALMS giving 2.5%**
SAWN	**Fasting month of RAMADAN.**
	Daylight fasting
HAJJ	**PILGRIMAGE to Mecca.**

The primitive conditions and discomforts of intensive living which I had to share with the pilgrims on my first voyage was a revelation. I became debilitated and felt suffocated from the extremely high humidity and the intense heat. I suffered as if I were permanently running a high temperature. When the body temperature is no longer under control and rises unduly then one is suffering from heat exhaustion. Living seemed to be an existence bordering on that condition. To add to my discomfort, which already appeared appalling, I went down with typhoid. That was when, medically, I really had a high temperature and I felt sufficiently unwell to question my survival. This is a time when one needs to have a belief of some kind which helps one to win through. I was sustained by thoughts of my folks at home and the will to see again my homeland.

When the influx of many passengers became imminent, and problems of disease threatened, then our ship was required to carry a doctor. At the same time, I was advised to have vaccinations, one of these being anti-typhoid. Unfortunately, the doctor did not come up to our European standards and he suffered from a condition known locally as elephantiasis. His leg was enormous and swollen. It was in fact very thick and had the semblance of an elephant's leg. Similarly, he had a gigantic foot which was wrapped in an improvised shoe covering. This he had to shuffle along the deck in front of him in a painful stumbling gait. To add to his discomfort he was almost blind. When he drew up the injections in the syringe, he did so using an eye piece, similar to that used by a jeweller or watch repairer. Without this degree of magnification he couldn't see the contents of the syringe. I subsequently believed that he had overdosed me and thus I succumbed to the disease.

He was a kindly fellow, despite his physical inadequacies. When I was in the throes of typhoid and confined to bed, he showed considerable concern. He gave me a valued tin of condensed milk. This, as you might suspect, was medication at a primitive level!

On the other-hand, I could not claim to be well fed, since my diet was solely the native curries. Perhaps I did derive some benefit, at least I am here to relate these events and I did escape that coffin with its hinged bottom.

Deaths averaged at least one per day and of course we could not have sufficient coffins to cope with these losses. At the stern of the ship the body, wrapped in a white shroud, was placed in the coffin. A fire bar was tied to the back of the corpse so that it would sink readily. The ship was stopped and turned to face Mecca. After the ceremony to bury the dead had been carried out then the coffin was swung out on its davit and by pulling a cord the hinged bottom of the coffin swung open to allow the body to drop into the sea. We retained the coffin which was repeatedly used in this way.

The Red Sea is brilliantly clear and is illuminated by the bright tropical sun overhead. Thus a prolonged view of the descending corpse could be seen, as it sank slowly and silently, eerily weaving its way down into the depths. The whiteness of the shroud was a pronounced tracer which could be seen for a long way down, as it gradually sank lower and lower into the sea, until it was hidden and lost in the obscurity of the deep. The ship was stopped whilst the burial ceremony took place. We then we proceeded under way, as quickly as possible, without committing the offence of moving off with unsympathetic haste. It was realised that there were many sharks in those waters and there could be nothing more distressing than to see the loved one being torn apart by sharks. Thus we would start engines immediately after release of the body, so that we might leave the spot far astern as soon as possible, believing this to be the wisest alternative.

Although the conditions on board were crowded and could have resulted in pushing and shoving this did not happen. There was an atmosphere of tolerance and peace as the pilgrims carefully made their way to and from the shops and latrines. Overall, religious fervour was pervasive, so prayers and patience accompanied good behaviour and peace. At sunrise, the Muezzin would call them to prayers, each phrase ending with the familiar "Alluha Akbar," (God is Great.) There was a large wooden arrow, ten foot long, which we kept pointing in the direction of Mecca. This enabled the pilgrims to face the holy city as they knelt and prostrated themselves in prayer. Five times every day, they performed these devotions and it was a remarkable sight. Arched backs, bowing in unison, formed a uniformly human mass, covering the entire deck areas of the ship. Thus 400ft long and 50ft wide, our two long decks were solid with pilgrims raising and lowering themselves, in harmony together, in ritual devotion.

At sunrise there were other sounds as they arose to perform their ablutions. Unfortunately this included a series of retching and spitting as they cleared their throats with a short piece of wood the "miswak." This piece of soft wood was used to clean their teeth but it was also pushed towards the back of the throat to help in coughing up phlegm. The obnoxious sounds which the retching and gurgling produced were indescribable. There was a standpipe adjacent to my cabin and the gurgling noises, surrounding these water points, generated by a thousand throats, was an inappropriate appetiser for breakfast. The spitting which followed was indiscreet and flew anywhere, everywhere, but not overboard!

Other rules of hygiene, which were broken, could be illustrated by the example of peeling an orange. The peel was simply dropped on to the deck wherever the orange was being eaten. Leaning over the ship's rail it would have been simple to drop the peel into the sea but this option was not considered. Rubbish containers failed to attract waste materials. Probably, with village life, this cultural approach was appropriate because sacred cows, roaming free, would expect fruit skins as part of their grazing and fodder. However, on board ship, over the period of ten days, the debris which could accumulate was substantial.

The congestion on the ship was exacerbated by the luggage and extra items which accompanied each passenger. Many carried an umbrella as a shade against the unrelenting sun. Passengers might also have their "chatti." This was an earthenware water container. As water filtered out of the minute pores of the vessel, it evaporated in the sun, and in doing so, it cooled the contents of the chatti. Sometimes, it would be a goat skin which was used as the water container.(mussuk) Naturally, a change of clothing would be available, especially the virgin white attire required when disembarking at the Holy Land. Also, there were the rugs or rush mats kept for use as a base on which to sleep or sit.

First stop was a temporary halt at Kamaran Island just inside the Red Sea. A doctor came out to the ship to ensure that the passengers would not import disease to Arabia. Yellow Fever, for example, was a threat for which we required clearance by the doctor, before we could proceed to land our pilgrims at Jeddah. We flew the yellow "Q" flag, indicating that we required a doctor to issue free practique.(disease clearance)

Whilst anchored off the island, a host of small boys swam alongside the ship and dived for coins thrown overboard. They demonstrated incredible skills, diving to great depths, forty to sixty feet down, to retrieve the coins. Admittedly, the water was crystal clear but they stayed under in excess of a minute, and at those depths, this was quite remarkable.

The recovered coins were held in their mouths, since they were virtually naked and had no pockets available. Beholding them dive with bulging cheeks, clenching the coins in their mouths, surpassed amazement. The passengers were entertained by the shouts and antics of the boys in the water but it was their feats of endurance which fascinated me. They were diving and swimming well out from the shore throughout the long period as we lay at anchor.

Also, this interval was an opportunity for shopping by the

passengers who were anxious to purchase chickens and fruit after suitable bartering. These items were quickly hauled up by rope from the canoes, but amazingly, nothing flew out of the baskets. Swarming passengers looked over the ships rails, whilst down below the shouts of trading from the Arabs in the boats created a lively interlude. Quite soon, we were granted free pratique which relieved us of any quarantine. We had no notifiable diseases on board. Thus we proceeded again on our way.

Arriving at Jeddah, the port of disembarkation for Mecca, we anchored close to the shore as there was neither a harbour nor berthing facilities. The pilgrims would be ferried ashore in small sailing boats. When they reached the shore, a remote desert village was all that would be seen.

As we dropped anchor at Jeddah, immediately there were Arabs bounding aboard taking names of pilgrims and trying to book up passengers before their competitors. The sailing boats were bumping one another, jostling to reach the gangway. Keen competition resulted and sometimes the rope of the competitor's boat would be released so that it drifted away. It was then difficult to return and find a space alongside our gangway. Tempers frayed and there was fighting and shouting amongst the boatmen as they jostled for position to board their passengers. This contrasted sharply with the religious demeanour and peaceful behaviour of the pilgrims.

We found the whole scene quite fascinating although some of the entertainment was both lively and exciting. It was spellbinding, witnessing the grossly overloaded boats, with gunnels virtually level with the water, struggling, precariously, towards the shore. The boats rocked alarmingly and only just escaped sinking as frightened passengers were told to keep still. The alternative was to hope that they could swim.

Prior to going ashore, pilgrims carried out ablutions; an all over wash was followed by the shaving of head, armpits and pubic area. Finally moustaches, beard and nails were trimmed. Barbers operated ashore in the streets to assist those pilgrims travelling overland.

Stepping ashore at Jeddah, pilgrims donned virgin white clothing reserved for this important moment. Symbolically, it denoted chastity. Two lengths of seamless white cloth were worn. One length was wrapped round the body from midriff to the knees. The other was thrown around the torso so that it partly covered the left shoulder, the back and the chest. This denoted that they had entered the Holy State of "Ihram." The word refers both to the garment and the special duties it imposes on the pilgrim. It is the symbol of the search for purity and mark of chastity. It was then forbidden to display jewellery and sex was prohibited. Pilgrims should avoid arguments, aggressive behaviour, blasphemy and evil. Thus they would proceed onwards on the pilgrimage towards Mecca and the Most Sacred Mosque.

It is of course forbidden for non-Muslims to be even within the vicinity of the holy city of Mecca, since the entire city is sacred territory. Intruders would meet with the certain penalty of death.
Pilgrims find that it is a long dry walk on a dusty desert track before they reach Mecca. The blazing hot sun reigns overhead and burns down on those walking throughout that punishing fifty mile trek. Some will suffer pillage and hardship with water sold to them at exorbitant prices. Naturally, the Arabs regard the pilgrims as a lucrative source of income to be exploited, since this comes but once per year.

PILGRIMAGE TO MECCA AND THE SACRED MOSQUE.
The "Hajj" is the most important contribution to Islam. It preserves for ever the bond between all forms of Islam. It is obligatory, spectacular and unifying. "Dhul Hijja." is the time of the lunar year for the Hajj which takes place between the ninth and twelfth day of the twelfth lunar month.

Within the Sacred Mosque there is the devotional epicentre, a cube shaped building, which is sixteen metres in height. This is the "KAABA" and is the House of ALLAH (Alkabah). Every mosque has a Kiblah (altar) indicating the direction of the Kaaba and focus of prayers.

MECCA is set in hot arid countryside, surrounded by barren hills. Every thoroughfare and passageway in the city is packed with pilgrims and is a veritable seething sea of the faithful, as they pour onwards, to make their way to the Sacred Mosque. Unlike Rome or Jerusalem, Mecca is proscribed to non-Muslims since Mohammed took the city for Islam in 630AD. It is set in an amphitheatre of hills fifty miles inland from the Red Sea port of Jeddah. At a fixed point of the lunar year, pilgrims converge on Mecca.

This means that since the lunar year loses eleven days annually, "Dhul-Hijja", the sacred month, moves around our calendar year. Unfortunately, at the time I was involved, it coincided with the hottest month of the year, burning August. This would occur every thirty-three years in comparison with our calendar.
The year of 570.AD. marked the birth of Mohammed. On the 8th June 632.AD. he died peacefully at Medina where a green dome was erected in 1860 over his tomb. The Koran is a collection of his revelations received from God in a cave on mount Hira. His last major act was to make the pilgrimage to Mecca. . "Oh People, God commands you to make this pilgrimage to this house so that he may reward you with Paradise and save you from the torment of hell."

The city of Mecca offers little in the mode of art or monumental architecture yet its magnetism draws Muslims in millions world wide. No other sacred site generates such fervour or emotional attraction. Mecca can be said to exert a stronger hold over more human emotions than any other single place on earth. Muslims in hundreds of millions prostrate themselves, facing Mecca five times every day, acknowledging the holy city and its devotional epicentre, the Kaaba, as Islam's "kiblah" or focus of prayer. The Kaaba or stone cube set in the centre of the Sacred Mosque is the holiest of holy and the nexus of the zealously held faith.

The Kaaba owes its name to the Arabic word for cube or dice. It is an almost square temple of granite blocks which is covered by a silk embroidered black cloth. A circular black stone at the site was said to have come from heaven and the angel Gabriele. Possibly it was a meteorite. The space or quadrangle about the Kaaba is capable of holding half a million worshippers. Throughout every hour of the day and night men and women walk round the Kaaba anti clockwise in worship. The prophet Mohammed delivered God`s command "Turn then thy face in the direction of the Sacred Mosque wherever you are, five times each day in prayer." One quarter of the Earth`s population responds in this way. Grey beards from minarets call Muslims to prayer before dawn lights the east and the last call each day is at sunset. Mecca becomes the one spot on the planet that each Muslim, whatever his nationality, aspires to visit at least once before his death. The Pilgrimage incorporates certain rituals and upon arrival in Arabia they proceed to the Sacred Mosque.

At last, they set eyes upon the mosaic marble of the two tall minarets positioned on either side of the Gate of Peace. They pass between them and enter the Sacred Mosque. Behold the incredible view of the Kaaba amidst waves of weaving worshippers who completely fill the surrounding quadrangle. It is a breathtaking sight. Many are overcome with emotion at this point. They raise their hands crying out, "Oh God you are peace and peace comes from you, so greet us oh our Lord with peace." The Kaaba is in the centre of the quadrangle and is surrounded by a solid mass of devotees. They have to walk in a counter clockwise direction to make seven circuits around the Kaaba. It is a time of intense emotional fervour as they perform the rituals of the Hajj.

Pilgrim buffet shop.

Monkey Island. ss.Khosrou

Centre of Jeddah

Diving for coins at Kamaran

WALKING   Pilgrims perform the TAWAF seven counter clockwise circuits walking around the Kaaba.

RUNNING   Between two hills Shaafa and Marwa 200 yards apart. This represents Patience and Perseverance.

PURIFICATION   Drink water from the sacred Zem Zem well.

STANDING   Demonstration of Faith on plains of Arafat.

FEAST OF SACRIFICE   The major holiday of the Islamic year.

The crux of the Hajj is the standing or mass assembly on the slopes of Mount Arafat. This is on the ninth day of Dhul-Hijja and begins when the sun reaches its zenith and lasts until sunset. It is the most impressive demonstration of faith to be witnessed on the face of the earth. This is followed by the "Stoning of the Devil."
Stones are gathered and hurled at three whitewashed figures. This symbolises the pilgrims' rejection of evil. As they throw each stone they cry out, "Allahu Akbar!" (God is most great.)

The Feast of Sacrifice is the culmination of the Hajj. It is also the major holiday in the Islamic year. Thereafter, there is a final fare-well visit to Mecca and perhaps also a visit to the Green Dome at Medina to pay respects at the tomb of Mohammed.

When the Pilgrims had completed the Hajj they returned on board and we voyaged back to Bombay. Disembarking the pilgrims they dispersed to return to a heroic welcome in their villages and homes. Now they would be revered as "Hajji Sahibs." This is akin to our respects for having gained a knighthood. Often the hair of the Hajji would be dyed red with henna to denote the newly acquired status. The respect shown to my Second Sparks, therefore, was not surprising. He had red hair which few villagers

Bunkering, Bombay. Coolies carrying coal in baskets on their heads.

Pilgrims
In
Ritual
prayer.

Pilgrims disembarking at Jeddah.

would ever have encountered. Thus occasionally they would addressed him as, "Hajji Sahib!"

When the pilgrims had departed, the decks and the ship were then thoroughly hosed down. This took care of the debris which inevitably was strewn about and particularly the insect life. When the passengers removed their belongings and rush mats, the insects darted out from under these hiding covers to find a new residence elsewhere. Unfortunately, our cabins then came under attack and it was a welcome relief to have a liberal deluge of water upon the insects, as a deterrent or preferably a death sentence. The accumulated particles of intensive living were also washed overboard to render us shipshape. Nevertheless, we had to suffer, in the first few hours, from the migrating 'Bombay Canaries' which entered our cabins and tried to persuade us that they could be suitable companions. Our venomous vigilance convinced them otherwise and peace and cleanliness soon ruled refreshingly over every surface on the ship.
An enormous relief to have silence and respite from all those crowding bodies. When I made my way from my cabin to the wireless room, it was a distance of only twenty feet, I had to step over at least a dozen bodies en route and now they were gone. The journey to the dining saloon was absolutely stifling as I joined a slow sweaty shuffle being nudged along held tightly packed within a crowd until the saloon was reached. The hope was that this crowd would continue to move, so that eventually without pushing, I could extricate myself. Returning to my cabin it was again, sweat and squeeze, nudge and shuffle, hoping all the time that I wouldn't pass out in the suffocating heat or collapse through lack of air. That was why this freedom from the multitude of bodies was such a glorious relief. The air was again oxygenated: it smelt sweet and not of malodorous body sweat. The disappearance of the insects was a further bonus.

We continued in the pilgrim trade, making several voyages to Jeddah and eventually bringing all our pilgrims back to India. This covered a five to six month period, our final voyage being around the Christmas of 1945. We left Jeddah on Christmas Eve. Thus, Christmas, my birthday and New Year were subdued events submerged in oppressive conditions of heat and bodies and overwhelmed by the multitude. It was not an atmosphere for any semblance of good cheer. Life does have its contrasts and none more dramatic than to compare this Christmas and birthday with last year's enjoyable celebrations amongst my friends in Alabahma. Fortunately, I was overtaken by events which briskly invaded our Wireless Telegraphy Operations. On the 30th December, the staccato Morse symbols, which I received, announced that war time restrictions on radio transmissions were no longer operative after 31st December, 1945. The task to resuscitate peace time wireless traffic now involved dusting off dormant ledgers and the perusal of volumes of regulations. I then concentrated on working out new traffic rates. The message confirmed that there would be 4.5d ship tax (approx 22p) and to add 100% surcharge. One commenced by counting the number of words in the message and multiplying by the price involved. This was based on international gold currency which was converted to sterling according to the exchange rate I would then apply the surcharge and convert the answer to rupees. This was a rather involved exercise until I became familiar with the calculations but with over one thousand passengers wishing to telegraph their expected time of arrival it was a hectic effort to complete all the forms and regulations.

I took in hand what I considered to be a reasonable number of telegrams and then had to wait until three days out from Bombay before the Radio Station ashore could be raised. When contact was made I discovered that they were not yet ready to undertake telegrams. I had to refund all the money taken to the original owners, an enterprise which was just part of the chaos and excitement. But despite everything, I was delighted to close with all balancing and in equilibrium. At least the challenge, of calculating the costs and working out a suitable price chart, had been a worthwhile exercise and rousted my dormant cerebrum.

One ghastly thought, which hovered over the forthcoming resumption of peace time operations, was the inevitable return to one Radio Officer per ship. Anticipation of the sad loss of my companion did not make its acceptance any more agreeable. Thus it was with regret that upon arrival in Bombay I lost my fellow sparks and had to soldier on alone.

The village of Jeddah, I was informed, was not worth the effort of struggling ashore and of course there was the inherent danger of encroaching upon the forbidden area for non believers. I had to be extra vigilant as a non Muslim. Curiosity is a persuasive driving force and it propelled me into a sailing craft for an adventurous visit to Jeddah. I discovered a primitive desert village which was devoid of any sanitation. This reminded me of the history of Edinburgh when the shout of, "Gardy loo!" (a corruption of the French "gardez l'eau") which meant, " Look out below!" because a bucket of foul water was about to be jettisoned. Thus I was vigilant of upper floor windows in case flying faeces had to be dodged. What could not be avoided, however, were the irritating flies which swarmed in clouds over the food displayed in the little market area. They buzzed and crawled all over my exposed skin, especially the moist areas around my mouth and eyes. It was not a pleasant experience considering the previous terrain of the flies was camel dung and the generally less than salubrious debris strewn over the ground.

Under the protection of my topi, I meandered about under a blistering sun with the feeling of heat rising slowly in waves from the sandy desert tracks. Weaving along the narrow streets, I found them just wide enough to allow the passage of a pedestrian or a donkey. I wandered between a variety of oddly shaped, crumbling houses. Nothing seemed to be upright, straight or vertical which simply meant upwards, whilst horizontally the passageways wound about in an irregular haphazard maze. As one walked along a track it suddenly narrowed to only four feet wide and as one looked up at the houses two stories high they practically touched at the top. Some of the leaning angles seemed unsafe and altogether it was fascinating to have visited this still primitive Arab village.

Sailing back out to the ship was virtually a journey through paradise. The dappled surface of the sea danced and sparkled with the bright sunshine as we trickled along. Pleasantly, our bow chuckled as it lapped the warm sea and the shallow bright water had the perfect clarity of crystal. Because of its rapid evaporation the salination of the Red Sea is noticeably increased and when hands were moistened by the buoyant sea, they dried encrusted with salt to illustrate the phenomena. Near the shore, the reefs were barely covered and as we proceeded, our gurgling craft cleft its way gently onwards to unravel the tropical pisciculture as down below our boat shoals of fish darted about in their limitless aquarium. Exotic brightly coloured fish were startled and little shoals darted about in the coral which itself was an amazing floral floor. Penetrating the surface of the sea revealed these creatures which are products of high temperatures and tropical sunshine. These natural attractions are appreciated but the environment of the Red Sea or on its shores I myself declare comfortable for the shortest visits only.

Port Sudan on the opposite side of the Red Sea was one of our ports of call. It was unbelievably hot and when combined with extremely high humidity the combination was stifling. Surely it must be one of the most uncomfortable places on earth. Certainly these lower reaches of the Red Sea have the highest wet bulb temperatures in the world and are distressingly oppressive. The area is tabled as unsuitable for the permanent settlement of 'Whites.' This is hardly surprising, with humidities in the nineties whilst temperatures hover around 115.F degrees. Profuse sweating combined with an absence of evaporation leaves one with the feeling of almost drowning or gasping for air in an overheated sauna in which one is trapped endlessly for days. I have lain exhausted on the upper boat deck with my nose out over the side hoping that I might find an upwards movement of air even if it were only the merest wisp.

We were in Port Sudan and the ship was loading cotton. Bear in mind, that throughout the war, it was unheard of ever to see any male with long hair. This was because our short back and sides was a product of the war when regulations in the Services demanded close cropped ultra short hair. Not only was this regarded as essential in the Armed Forces, but it was embedded in our culture, and we all felt that it was comfortable, smart and presumably more hygienic. One can imagine the consternation therefore, when the "Fuzzy Wuzzies" appeared and started loading the cotton bales. Never had I witnessed or even imagined such unbelievable heads of hair. I was astounded to see these dark natives, with muscular lithe bodies, sporting what looked like a busby worn permanently as headgear. Their hair was densely thick and extremely long. It dangled down the back of their necks forming into lumps clotted together with waste. These matted clumps of hair swung like beads down the back of their heads. It both looked and smelled as if it had been coated with camel dung. Probably cocoa nut oil was applied as a hair dressing, which then collected accumulations of dust and debris. A piece of wood, with an end like a pronged fork, was inserted into the hair in the fashion of a comb. It may have been used as a comb but in practice it gave some relief by scratching and disturbing the biting insect life. The smell was quite appalling and I found myself itching and scratching my head, induced no doubt through auto-suggestion. The phenomena of this ultra long thick hair so surprised me, that immediately, I dashed for my camera. This was an opportunity not to be missed, as my camera was now permitted after its prohibition throughout the war.

I spotted one of these workers on board and was carefully taking aim with the camera, to record this amazing sight for posterity, when, suddenly, he lunged towards me. Rather obviously, the situation was dangerous. I became immediately aware of impending disaster. His anger had erupted instantly. He seemed to have gone wild. The whites of his wide eyes glared at me as he flailed his long arms. He had enormous hands clenched into hammer like fists and they were fast approaching the target of his fury. With no time for explanations, I turned and in flustered haste, picked up speed as quickly as possible to distance myself from this pounding threat. He sped after me but my knowledge of the ship enabled me to dodge out of sight and escape momentarily.

It transpired that in his opinion I was capturing his image and spirit and this was a taboo worth defending unto the death. Had he seen me again it would have been my demise or at the very least the destruction of my camera. I was not prepared to confront him or even to think about negotiations. Apart from his wild appearance and mood, he was over six feet tall. These Fuzzy Wuzzy fellows are impressive figures being both menacingly tall and expressing aggression. They look wild, unkempt, and threatening even before being provoked or incited to kill. In fact, for my own survival and safety, I had to remain hidden for two days whilst this giant worked on board, still seeking the recovery of his spirit or the death of his perpetrator.

Resumption of our normal cargo passenger business allowed some respite and we escaped out of the tropics. I found new energy so that it became opportune to contemplate more distant excursions ashore, as next we called at Suez.

I arose at 5.30am to catch the train to Cairo partaking breakfast at a large Naafi canteen. Later that morning, refreshed and breakfasted, I hailed a taxi and we headed for the Pyramids. Soon I was on horseback, which is what is likely to happen if your companion favours that mode of transport. Normally, it would be a fifteen minute walk to the Pyramids but with my teeth rattling I was there in under two minutes. Possibly, had I given the Arab horse owner a bigger tip, he would not have whipped the horse's rear flank so vigorously and procedure would have been more stylish. I held on despite lack of horsemanship and demonstrated at least I was not a pushover nor easily intimidated for baksheesh.

It is obvious why one would wish to view these prodigious and enduring monuments in stone for they date back almost to 3000 years B.C., reach heights of about 140 metres and have sides as much as 230 metres at the base. Constructed of blocks of stone, the largest up to thirteen and a half metres long and weighing 163,000 kilos, these are the staggering statistics which confront the onlooker. Similarly, the engineering feats of construction, in those past ages, is quite bewildering. These geometrically shaped tumuli of masonry were erected over royal burials and within them, chambers were constructed as temple or funerary areas.

After visiting the Pyramids we viewed the Sphinx which is partly man made and part natural. The blocks of stone in its construction were excavated from limestone quarries to the north. These blocks were shaped into a leonine body with a human head, resembling Chephren. It is twenty metres in height and fifty-seven metres in length. The Sphinx is representative of the divine nature of the king as the solar divinity was believed to manifest himself in the lion and the king.

These wonders of the world were enjoyed and we had a fascinating day. Not least was the gauntlet run with the hordes of touts, with demands for baksheesh (meaning alms in Arabic). These started with money demanded for sugar for the horse, or else! Then followed a constant stream of 'guides' and 'watchmen,' with demands for money for a torch, whilst others pursued us with requests to buy a priceless object which had just been secretly excavated. They hovered like mosquitoes and homed in with their insatiable demands.

In Cairo, the urchins although much younger, were still of a predatory nature. The ability to surreptitiously remove a wrist watch swiftly and unnoticed would amaze any magician or pickpocket.

Knowing some of these ruses I kept temptations out of sight. The thieves were also adept at removing pens from pockets using a newspaper but again this was prevented by not having such items in view. However, I realised that I had been duped when one young lad pointed to the large dollop of cream polish on my shoe. This had been daubed on by his accomplice, a few yards earlier and now there was no alternative but to have a shoe shine to remove it. After the shoe shine, one contemplated not paying but as he poured a liberal amount of crimson liquid on to his brush and threatened to swish it all over my uniform, 'baksheesh' was the diplomatic answer.

In the zoo, bananas to feed the zebras or fish for the seals, were pressed on me at a price. On the footpath, a spider was drawn in the dust, with demands to cover it with money, to hear of your fortune. On the train a tout had a solid gold diamond ring which he admitted stealing. He was most furtive as he kept looking over his shoulder in case he was discovered with the stolen property. He demonstrated the quality of the diamond by almost zipping open the glass window of our railway carriage as he scored across it. Certainly it must have been a genuine diamond and the ring was pure gold but in my wisdom, I hesitated to believe him and he did not make his sale. I understand that glass can be cut and shaped in such a way that it acts like a diamond but its sharp edges are soon blunted when given the treatment of our demonstrator.

If a man make a pilgrimage round Alexandria in the morning,
God will make for him a golden crown, set with pearls, perfumed
with musk and camphor, and shining from East to the West.
Ibn Duqmaq.

Continuing our travels, the **Khosrou** sailed into **Alexandria** which has a romantic past but unlike Athens has no ancient monuments, merely memories for the sightseer. Alexander the Great in 331 BC ordered the causeway to be contracted to join two ridges thus forming the city's two great harbours. It is the city where

Cleopatra committed suicide and there are many phantoms from its past. Because of the fresh sea breezes of the Mediterranean it has more of a sparkle than other Egyptian towns.

Our short stay in temperatures considerably cooler than those which we normally had to suffer, in my opinion, was delightfully refreshing. However, the Indian members of the crew declared that they had never been so cold as the temperature fell to around sixty-five degrees F. They could scarcely comprehend how my part of the world could be much colder. Apart from entertaining shows and delightful coffee houses where in the afternoons I enjoyed the exquisite Egyptian sweet meats and cakes, I recall only that this visit to Alexandria was both short and sweet.

The canal sailing was pleasant and we had a number of passengers who were sufficiently interesting to fuel the ship's gossip. People generally are worthy of attention but passengers on board ship are subjects for scrutiny. Knowledge of their complete history and pertinent details of current behaviour was freely exchanged as we officers conversed. As can be imagined we had some fascinating discussions throughout each voyage. However, having to live so close to the passengers I sometimes encountered problems. For example, a Muslim woman was in labour and about to give birth. The husband had erected a cotton screen to afford privacy but he had constructed it in such a way that the outside bulkhead of my cabin formed part of the enclave. Thus my port hole overlooked the secluded area. The woman was screaming in pain and obviously suffering but the husband would not permit our doctor to attend because he was a male. If I stood up in my cabin I could look out on the scene but I dare not be seen, otherwise I would have been guilty of intrusion and thus could expect the dire consequences. I became virtually a prisoner in an enclosure of panic, screaming, torture, and the contortions endured in that protracted birth which continued over two days. I am not sure who was the more relieved when the episode concluded with the appearance of the offspring. Unfortunately, although the noise abated it was

Fuzzy Wuzzy

Dhobi Wallahs

merely the volume which was reduced and the sounds only less excruciating.

On one occasion I had a group of noisy Indian musicians. They may have been entertainers but they were definitely not appreciated when I was trying to catch up on my sleep. I popped my head out of the cabin and suggested that they should stop as I was endeavouring to sleep. The music ceased but I soon awoke once more and could not have been pleased for I recall throwing a bucket of water over the leading musician in case he was not conversant with plain English. This dampened the entertainment and a drowsy interlude followed.

.Arriving in Bombay the *ss.Khosrou* had to undergo major repairs, involving the partial renewal of her wooden decks. I became ensconced in the club for Merchant Navy personnel situated in down town Bombay. The respite experienced with this change was unbelievable. Normally the docks, at a distance of five miles from town, involved a lot of walking. I frequently trudged wearily back to my ship in the early hours of the morning picking my way around the sleeping bodies in the streets. Half the population of Bombay live on the streets which, at night, become makeshift dormitories. I also had to be careful not to tread on the rats which freely scuttled to and fro as I wove my way back to the ship.

Despite the poverty in this city, which is probably also foremost in India for its display of wealth, there seemed to be no conflict. On reflection, it is quite remarkable that walking alone in the early hours of the morning in that environment, I felt perfectly at ease. It was the safest part of the world I had yet visited. Despite the juxta- position of poverty and wealth this explosive situation did not seem likely to detonate. I attributed this situation to the demeanour and gentle character of the Indian population reinforced by the culture of the Hindus.

Living down town eliminated the walk back to the ship. This was especially appreciated after attending an evening show. Just to slip into the club and retire to sleep in a genuine bed, instead of a bunk, was a blessing of undeniable luxury. Furthermore, the food was fantastic. I could scarcely recognise the beans which were green, as opposed to the customary black servings on the ship. This applied to all the vegetables and the range of meats with succulent flavours exploded with my delight. Tough curried mutton was our staple diet on board ship, varied only on Sundays, when chicken might appear. I now relished tender stew or steak, not fiercely curried so that the entire menu far exceeded any culinary experiences on board ship. Living ashore provided a break and a respite indeed, for which I was truly thankful. Ashore and relaxed I found time to contemplate my surroundings. The pompous Gateway of India Arch is the principal landmark for those visitors arriving in the deep water harbour of **Bombay.** It was built to welcome British Royalty and other dignitaries visiting India. It was erected adjacent to the water front Taj Mahal Hotel where the anticipated lavish accommodation was provided.

After 1857 when the British Raj took over from the East India Company they installed a professional Civil Service Administration and thereafter followed the proliferation of proud Victorian public buildings one of which is the celebrated Flora Fountain where water gushes from the statue of the Roman Goddess of spring. The Victoria Terminus which is the pride of Bombay was built 1888. The swish Marine Drive along the waterfront was developed and became known as the Queen's Necklace because of its sparkling lights at night.

At the top of Malabar Hill I visited the hanging gardens and the"Towers of Silence." This is where the Parsee believers place their dead to be devoured by vultures. The adjacent topiary gardens display turkey, hen and elephant shapes skilfully crafted out of shrubs of box wood . Viewing these gardens occupied an amusing and pleasant afternoon. I had always been fascinated by the influences of the proud British and their supercilious style in

Poona, by Gad Sir! often portrayed by sketches humorously depicting the British despotism in India. Somehow, I was fascinated by the implied humour and pompous behaviour of the personnel at this military hill station. Thus I embarked on a four hour journey by train to Poona to investigate this curiosity.

The journey was 119 miles in an overcrowded steam train with stops numerous enough to make the rattling slow journey very tedious. **Poona** is two towns in one, the old city and the military cantonment. The original military camp had developed into a separate entity with its own shopping centre, banks and amusements. It is a pleasant town with wide tree-lined roads and sufficient shops and cinemas to make army life in the absence of home a little easier to bear. As a typical Indian village, Poona itself was more crowded but the absence of transport was noticeable when accustomed to down town conditions in Bombay.

I hired a bicycle to investigate both towns but it proved to be a parched, dry ride and the timing was inopportune since we were in the hot season. As a hill station 1850 ft above sea level it was supposed to be cooler than steamy Bombay. In fact, it was gasping hot and dust dry. I could feel the heat bouncing off the roadway and rising to dry out my nostrils to the point where they almost stuck together. My exertions soon resulted in my mouth and throat becoming thoroughly parched and stick dry. I would love to have been able to plunge my face into water just to alleviate these symptoms. My reluctance to drink from doubtful water supplies aggravated my dehydration until eventually I was forced to purchase water from an itinerant Pani Wallah, thus risking Delhi Belly or worse. Mad dog of an Englishman should not have been riding around at that time of day nor at that time of year. Prying into the aura of the sahibs and memsahibs in their Poona habitat provided a fine excuse for this excursion but it could have been enjoyable with more appropriate timing. I had envisaged stopping overnight but decided to return to Bombay that same day. My curiosity was vindicated but not entirely because the conception I had had of Poona, in effect, seemed now to have been only music hall banter and I was the victim of a joke.

Elephanta Island, a short boat journey from Bombay, is a tourist attraction and hides a classic millennium cave temple. Statuesque arrangements could be viewed in the subdued light which filtered down through crevices into the caves, creating an impressive atmosphere which left me with an afternoon of memories and made this mystical interlude worthwhile. Juhu was the subject of my next sortie. Situated some twenty miles from Bombay, it had a fine tropical beach with popular week-end cottages. It was hardly surprising that a group of RAF personnel was lounging on the beach and lapping up their stay in India, although this environment was an enclave quite remote from the India with which I was familiar.

SS.RIZWANI
A summons to the Marconi office ended further reflections upon life around Bombay as I learned of a new appointment to the *SS RIZWANI*. This was another ship of the Mogul line and slightly larger at 5448 Grt. It had extra passengers and additional cabin accommodation but the main deck was more enclosed and lack of air movement meant greater discomfort and distinctly hotter conditions living on board this ship. The contrast was noticeable after the comforts in the stone buildings of Bombay. Hot decks and sizzling metal sides of the ship created the impression of living in a corrugated iron hut, despite the surrounding sea.

The manager in the Marconi office asked me to do him a favour. On behalf of his friend, there was a package which he would appreciate being taken to Greece. The Greeks were starving as a result of the war and there was a shortage of clothing. The package would help to alleviate these sufferings. Problems with customs had been overcome and everything had been arranged so that someone would collect the parcel upon the ship's arrival. I agreed to help out in the circumstances but even the 1st Mate was

173

devastated and alarmed when he had to swing out a derrick over a barge alongside our ship to lift a huge packing crate on board. Both he and I expected a brown paper parcel which one could carry. We were ready to sail and this delay, coupled with the size of the package, courted some curses and his distinct annoyance. I now feared the reactions of the customs in Greece when confronted with this large package. If I were questioned upon arrival I had neither information about the sender nor the recipient and of course I had little understanding about the contents. Today in a climate of drug trafficking perhaps I would have been more circumspect. At least I could sympathise with those who are duped, as innocents, and are caught out unawares.

The First Mate, fortunately, was a quiet retiring introspective type of person unlikely to make a fuss. At this moment, he was besotted with the love of his life whom he had just married. Tearing himself away on this voyage left him heartbroken and in torture as he pined and yearned for his love every second of every day of their separation. He punished himself endlessly by playing Cole Porter's "Night And Day" on his gramophone.

> *Night and day you are the one*
> *Only you beneath the moon*
> *and under the sun.*
> *Whether near to me or far,*
> *It's no matter, darling, where you are*
> *I think of you night and day.*
> *Day and night, why is it so*
> *That this longing for you follows*
> *wherever I go?*
> *In the roaring traffic's boom*
> *In the silence of my lonely room,*
> *I think of you, night and day.*
>
> *Night and day under the hide of me,*
> *There's an oh, such a hungry*

yearning, burning inside of me.
And its torment won't be through
Till you let me spend my life
making love to you
Day and night, night and day.

These sounds were from a man who was obsessed and visibly heartbroken and as his musical lamentations drifted out from his cabin, I could not help sympathising with the poor fellow. I had no alternative because the gramophone played unceasingly until I became enraptured in its mood as the melody penetrated under my hide night and day. It was hauntingly beautiful to feel the tropical breeze, as night and day she was the one, as we sailed along beneath the moon and under the sun. With the waves lapping gently, we became entwined intensely, day and night, night and day.

Memories, recalled by that haunting melody, are rekindled whenever I hear that song. I have been imprinted with the magic of his gramophone and its music which immediately transports me to Indian waters on board the 'Rizwani.' That song "Night and Day" together with "The Road to Mandalay" exude the magic that is, for me, the spell of India.

The nearer we approached our destination with the package the more alarming grew the situation. I did not know what the box contained nor to whom it was destined. I had taken it on trust and already the Mate was asking awkward questions and wondering why he had listened to me about conveying the ten foot by eight foot crate. Did it contain contraband, guns or drugs? What would the custom inspectors say and how would we extricate ourselves? It was not listed as cargo and that was a further complication requiring explanation. I might be in deep trouble but could only await for events to unfold. The alternative was to surreptitiously drop it overboard but it was too large to disappear unseen and it might even float so that we would be in trouble for endangering

KARACHI.

PARSEE TOWER OF SILENCE.

TAJ - MAHAL HOTEL. BOMBAY.

shipping.

We dropped anchor in the bay outside Piraeus harbour. A launch came out and asked about the parcel which was under my guard. The 1st Mate eagerly swung the crate out and overboard, with what I felt to be undue efficiency and haste. Incredibly, it vanished on to the launch with no further questions being asked. Possibly higher authorities had sanctioned its conveyance and it was likely that baksheesh had oiled the negotiations although I myself received no financial inducement. I no longer cared but what did jar my conscience was the sight of numerous rotund, well attired Greek inhabitants in better conditions than our own folks would be back home. There was little evidence of deprivations and there seemed to be no shortage of luxuries or food. Furthermore, the abundance of rich cream cakes and lavishly iced confectionery made me resolve never again to be a victim of good intent, especially when backed by false pretences. Admittedly, the port of Piraeus had been blown to pieces and buildings were in ruins because of ships exploding in the harbour but the sufferings of the population ashore did not compare even marginally with citizens of Malta or the rationing and bombing back home.

I had now time to explore. It was not the sleazy water-front of **Piraeus** which beckoned but the aesthetic architectural past of Athens and Attica. The history going back to mythological kings and the buildings of renown were factors worthy of my time and this was very limited.

Athens was at its zenith 480BC at which time Socrates could have been encountered when shopping in the city and one could have looked up to see the Acropolis under construction. This became the most famous building in Europe and amongst others provided employment for Athenians who were set to work to improve their city. Artists strove to excel themselves in the beauty of their workmanship but buildings were still unfinished when the Peloponnesian War with Sparta broke out in 431BC. Subsequent wars and upheavals, including the period when the Turks installed a garrison in the Acropolis, brought about the decline of the edifices. Even the Parthenon, one of the more famous ruins in Athens, lost its choice objects and sculpted frieze when Lord Elgin carted them off to grace his home. He subsequently sold them to the British Museum when he became financially embarrassed. The Greeks currently are seeking the return of the "Marbles" and continue to raise this contentious matter.

Because of our short stay I merely glimpsed at these ruins and remains of the ancient city and fort of the Acropolis. After a brief visit to the Parthenon, Olympeum and surrounds we were again on our way. I found the city of Athens beautiful and fascinating and with its historical and artistic past it merited more time than our one day visit allowed. Its present Venuses perambulating the sidewalks also deserved my attention and had it not been for most of our passengers being returning Greek refugees I would have missed out entirely on these beauties of modern Greece.

In Alexandria I bought a portable typewriter to assist with my daily recording of current news, received from Morse transmissions. I normally produced the ship's "News Bulletin" which was then displayed for all to peruse but my handwriting was not the most legible script. This was hardly surprising since the speed of Morse being received was marginally faster than one could write. Thus I learned to touch type and took down the Morse directly on the typewriter. The expertise required to achieve these operations fulfilled job satisfaction and emphasised my status as "News Reporter" of world events.

Jeddah, Port Sudan and Aden were visited as our ports of call en route back to Bombay. The temperatures on board ship were already soaring and as the weeks went by progressively we were beginning to dissolve in our sweat. I needed little convincing that the next voyage on this ship would be stifling and insufferable. We were due to restart with our passengers for the Hajj and we would be encountering the burning month of August in this hell hole of the Red Sea. I had now spent well over a year from home and had been promised to be relieved upon my return to Bombay. I was determined not to be involved with another exhausting voyage on this ship. Already I had lost over two stones in weight and the combined effects of diet and environment had undermined my health. Recurring bouts of malaria did not help. The food was substandard even for these ships and rather surprisingly it even resulted in a strike. When we reached Bombay the entire crew refused to sail again with the "Butler" who was responsible for our food and menu. He was the equivalent of the chief steward on British ships but he wielded more power and even chief officers had been known to succumb to the authority which he used when arguments arose about his victualling. The outcome of the present complaints for the first time ever, resulted in the Butler being dismissed which explains why on this ship criticism of our food was more than justified.

The present voyage returning to Bombay was already proving to be too hot for comfort, particularly in my cabin which was down on the main deck. It was even less attractive than sleeping out up top on the boat deck. At least up on that deck I could imagine there was a light wafting of air as I desperately gasped for oxygen. The air was entirely vitiated and this airless sensation was due to its very high humidity and the congested conditions on board. At least up on the open boat deck I would not be stifled by the crowds in the fetid living areas. The passengers were not permitted access to the upper boat deck.

Having considered my options, I decided to sleep out on deck for greater comfort and I rented my cabin to a passenger. I had heard of cabins being rented out to passengers but always accompanied with stories about the resulting devastation and rubbish left as remains in the cabin. In fact the putrid smell on one occasion was a corpse found in the wardrobe, dumped together with human excrement. That of course was an unlikely tale, I told myself, and the sort of exaggeration which I was prepared to take with scepticism. Bearing in mind, rumours frequently have elements of truth, I imagined that there would be associated problems. There was on the otherhand the financial inducement amounting to almost six months salary. Thus I was sorely tempted. Anyway I vowed that this would be my final voyage so I decided to take the risk.

Of course the new occupant of my cabin had friends and it was incredible to see how many were involved in our supposedly secret lucrative arrangement. They piled into my cabin and each in turn smoked the hubble bubble pipe which was passed round as they made themselves at home. The smell of rubbish and debris was disgusting and seemed to increase each day. I became worried about the outcome especially with the number of inhabitants who had become involved.

I did receive my revenue but I needed plenty baksheesh at the end of the voyage to encourage my 'boy' to thoroughly clean up my cabin. There were no bodies left but I had to be generous to ensure that my 'boy' carried out a "pukkah sougie" (proper wash) Anything less would have meant the cabin being uninhabitable. At least I would not have to concern myself with the lingering aromas since I had no intention of being present for the next voyage. At the same time I was not abandoning the type of situation which I myself encountered when I first boarded with a bug ridden accommodation.

12

ROUNDING THE WORLD

On arrival in Bombay the problems of finding my replacement perturbed me more with each day that I waited. Every call which I made to the Marconi Office resulted in more excuses. Finally I took a stance and completely refused to sail again on the ship. It was now or never. The situation was especially difficult because already two Radio Officers had resigned when appointments were suggested to ships permanently on the Coast. With 'Pilgrim' ships the problems trebled. Fortunately, the radio officer from the *mv.Daghestan* was induced to accept an appointment to a passenger ship. He may have been deluded by the 'passenger status' of the ship and the sweet talking of the Marconi manager but that was not my concern. The *ss. Rizwani* would, indeed, be a revelation but at least my exchange was achieved.

My problems were not yet quite over because when I checked over the wireless gear of my new set up aboard the *MV.DAGHESTAN* the captain was scornful as he hinted that the Direction Finder was of little use. I requested that it should therefore be calibrated and its accuracy checked. This meant that the ship would be delayed by an extra day and, not surprisingly, the captain declined to accept the extra costs which this would entail to the shipping company.

Possibly, since I was accustomed to having servants under my authority, over many months recently I quite naturally assumed an air of command. I dared to challenge the captain's view and demanded that these corrections were instituted. I told the captain that unless he had the equipment checked to my satisfaction then he should not expect me to operate it in future. If it were useless then it was the captain's responsibility, and not mine, because I was requesting the opportunity to put it into good order.

I doubtless seemed surprisingly arrogant and this stormy attitude created confusion but it did mean that I found facilities to check my Direction Finder equipment. Our lifeboat was reluctantly lowered into the water and using the lifeboat transmitter it circulated the ship whilst I received its signals and made a graph of deviating errors throughout the compass headings.

The ship was delayed for the entire day and the captain and his officers who were involved with this operation, were certainly not pleased. They had also been very friendly with the previous radio officer, whom I had deposed, so these were not good omens for establishing rapport with my new ship's officers.

It is perhaps difficult to understand the hierachy on board ship because there is no saluting and members of the Merchant Navy tend to operate in separate groups according to their work. Despite the absence of a distinct command structure, each vessel invariably runs smoothly. Of course the captain is in complete command of the entire ship and everybody on board but his authority is founded on the tradition of his job and respect for his experience. As Master with complete control, he can sometimes be over bearing. Usually, he is affectionately referred to as the "Old Man." He is, perhaps, the oldest person on the ship and is likely to have achieved the longest service at sea. A ship proceeds safely whilst out on the ocean but it is in danger whenever land is in sight. The captain always takes over the bridge when entering or leaving port. He is nominally on duty during the 'eight to twelve' watch both morning and evening. The Third Mate in fact stands this watch but since he is the junior officer, the captain is in effect looking over his shoulder to ensure that he operates the ship with safety.

The First Mate takes the 'four to eight' watch and as with the other navigation officers he spends these periods at sea on the bridge and in the wheelhouse. He controls the running of the ship and instructs the bosun on the tasks to be undertaken. He is also responsible for organising the maintenance of the ship including, rigging, painting and cargo handling.

The Second Mate when on duty is in charge of navigation and chartwork. He is on the 'twelve to four' watch and starts off with his sextant as he takes his noonday sight. The chronometer, which plays an important role in his calculations, is wound up by him each Sunday together with the other ship's clocks. The Sparks usually supplies the accurate updated time signal obtained by radio. Unfortunately, the Second Mate is relegated to the graveyard watch which is the midnight to four am. spell and the least favourable hours to be awake either during the night or having to work throughout siesta time of the afternoon.

Sometimes apprentice navigation officers are included in this structure. They join at sixteen years of age as cadets and with tuition at sea, together with studies, hope to pass exams to become third mate and climb to the rank of captain, eventually having their own command. The apprentices work under the instructions from the 1st Mate with daily routine work on deck supervised by the bosun.

The Bosun is the equivalent of the foreman ashore and he has about four A.B.s. under his control . These are the able bodied seamen who have passed various tests and served a required period at sea. The A.B.s. perform all general duties on deck such as painting, anchoring, rigging and derrick operations. They also take the helm in the wheelhouse on the bridge to steer the ship. The A.B.s. work a twenty-four watch between them whilst the bosun works throughout the day.

When entering or leaving port the captain is on the bridge with his first and second mate at the bow and stern of the ship, assisted by A.B.s. When loading or unloading the First Mate takes charge of these operations and especially the careful arrangements of stowing the cargo.

The Chief Engineer obviously is in charge of the ship's machinery and has several engineers under his control. The Second, Third and Fourth Engineers operate watches at times similar to the deck officers. There may be an additional fifth or sixth engineer depending upon the size of the ship. Also there is the donkeyman whose title originated from the latter days of sail when a small donkey engine became available to assist with the work of hauling. Hence the heaving shanty:

"Donkey Riding"

CH: ...*Way, hay, an' away we go!*
Donkey ridin', donkey ridin'!
Way, hay, an' away we go!
Oh, ridin' on a donkey!...

When in port the main engines were stopped. It was uneconomic to produce steam on the main boilers hence the use of a small donkey boiler to power a variety of auxiliary units like generators or winches. The donkeyman looked after these items. There would also be a greaser and in the case of coal burning vessels there would be three stokers who would maintain the fires necessary to keep up steam throughout each day and night.

Engineers are often very busy in port because that is the time when repairs and maintenance can be carried out. It is perhaps surprising that engineers never set foot on the bridge. Likewise, the Mates never enter the engine room unless emergency circumstances prompts their appearance and intrusion to these other sections. The different areas of the ship seem appropriate for the tasks of the officers or crew concerned, but strangely, each section of the ship is strictly territorial.

The chief Steward looks after the victualling and food supplies. He has one or two assistants so that one assistant steward would wait on the tables in the officers' saloon whilst the other would make up the officers' bunks and keep the cabins clean. The chief steward was also in charge of the cook and his cabin boy or assistant so that working together they ensured overall good house-keeping.

The Radio Officer was independent and practically free to roam being allied to none of these groups, although he was sometimes involved with navigation employing his Direction Finder in close co-operation with the navigation officers. I personally spent considerable time on the bridge because of my interest in navigation and the radio cabin was invariably very close to the chart room and is on the bridge of British ships. Also, war time duties required our presence on the bridge, assisting with flag signalling or morse signalling by light.

During the war we had three radio officers so that twenty-four hours continuous radio watch was maintained. When in peace time we reverted to one radio officer alone, then an automatic alarm system was adopted. This was set off by the transmission of four long dashes, each of four seconds' duration, with one second spaces. In emergencies, other ships or shore stations would activate the Automatic Alarm which would bring the radio operator into action since the alarm sounded in his radio room and the call was relayed to his cabin.

When leaving port I would send our 'TR' to the local coastal station. This announced our departure and destination and indicated that we were now on the air. Communications with foreign vessels or stations are facilitated by the use of the "Q" Code. QRD ? for example means "Where are you bound and where are you from ?" Other examples are "QRA ?" meaning "What is the name of your vessel (or station)?" We recognised coded groups for correspondence: "QRU ?" "Have you anything for me? " "QTC ?" "How many telegrams have you to send"? Or, of course, without the question mark it would be "QTC 4 " "I have four telegrams for you." Thus a series of questions or answers and advice may be internationally exchanged through our "Q" code abbreviations which range through the alphabet using QR-, QS-,QT-, and others to enable speedy exchange of commonly used information including phrases on "Distress", "Search and Rescue", and "Direction Finding."

It is amazing that once learned these "Q" coded signals can still be reeled off despite having rested unused for fifty years in a dormant section of my brain. Likewise, having learned "Morse" signals it is amazing that the rhythmic sounds are still readily interpreted despite languishing unheard for half a century. Admittedly, the speed of twenty characters per second has slowed down to perhaps sixteen but the ability of our brains is quite remarkable.

Ever since Jack Phillips, the radio officer of the ill fated **Titanic**, stayed at his post so long that he lost all chance of saving himself and went down with the ship, this devotion to duty was established as traditional amongst radio officers. 1400 radio officers were lost in the war representing one for every three ships.

1899 The first distress message was sent by radio from the *Goodwin Light ship* when it was run down and sinking. 1904 the "CQ" all stations call was adapted by Marconi operators to "CQD" as a signal to indicate a dangerous situation requiring immediate assistance. The public interpreted the letters to mean "Come Quick Danger." 1908 A general order was issued that "SOS" would be the international distress call. During World War Two "RRRR" indicated under attack from Armed Raider, "AAAA" being attacked by aircraft, "SSSS" attacked by submarine and usually STBD or PORT to indicate on which side the torpedo had struck to assist the escorts to locate the U.Boat.

Both CQD and SOS were used in the *Titanic* disaster, after which it became compulsory to have a radio operator on board so that no longer would a ship be isolated at sea when help might be just over the horizon.

Selfless devotion to duty was recognized with the posthumous award of the George Cross to Radio Officer David Broadfoot on the *Princess Victoria.* In 1953 she foundered in a storm while bound from Stranraer to Larne. The power of the seas stove in the steel rear doors of this Irish Sea ferry. Tragically 128 lives were lost including the radio officer who communicated with Port Patrick radio station right up to the point when the vessel was capsizing. He even apologized for his difficult Morse signals as he was transmitting whilst the ship was turning over. David Broadfoot lived in Morecambe. Sam Batte, the Port Patrick radio operator decided to make a simple memorial. He planted 128 snowdrop bulbs outside the radio station and form a "BNZN" the *Princess Victoria's* call sign. By 31st January each year, on the anniversary of the disaster, freshly blooming snowdrops on the green hillside clearly signal the memorial and poignant reminder to those who understand.

Nobody questioned how we operated or if we were efficient. Perhaps it was because of our conscientious application to our work that omissions or mistakes did not arise. We kept the hours required to ensure messages for the ship were received from the shore stations. This meant listening to the traffic lists to check if the ship's call sign appeared. This would indicate that the station had traffic either routeing orders or telegrams for the ship. We maintained radio watch on 500kc/s (600 metres) which was the distress or calling wavelength. Silence had to be observed from fifteen minutes to eighteen minutes past each hour and again at forty-five to forty-eight minutes past each hour. Transmissions on that wavelength during these silence periods were avoided so that distress signals and emergency traffic could be heard without morse sounds interfering. In fact the Radio Officer's clock had these silence periods shaded red to remind him of his radio silence observance.

In port we were free of duties because the main aerial system between the masts would be lowered to allow the cranes to work over the hatches. I was very happy to operate the Jolly Boat or lifeboat as a ferrying service for those wishing to go ashore. Sometimes I would collect mail or messages to oblige others who had duties on board. The ship's library was often left to the 'Sparks' and I was happy to control the lending and exchange of books on the ship or even their replacement from ashore. Independence and freedom were rights which were precious so perhaps that is why we were happy to apply our talents conscientiously and generously to other activities of our choice.

At sea we usually received orders by radio and sent our E.T.A. (expected time of arrival). Thus we kept the captain and the ship in touch with our agents ashore. Whilst listening on the air waves I logged each transmission heard perhaps every fifteen minutes and listened for the various traffic lists to check if messages or telegrams were on hand for our ship.

Weather bulletins and safety warnings were recorded and passed to the captain. As all Radio Officers were bound by a code of secrecy, the captain and I might be the only persons aware of the ship's movements announced through a Morse message. On a voluntary basis I produced a daily news bulletin which was greatly appreciated since radios had not yet proliferated on board ships. In war time they were forbidden in case their oscillations indicated their presence to prowling U.Boats.
On one ship after many weeks at sea without shore leave I listened to my colleagues complaining bitterly about the length of their

hair. "I will give you a trim if you like," I offered. The first desperate victim put his head on the block and I set to work. I had seen my father perform his magic on his sons so I was no stranger to the observation of this technique but I completely lacked any practical experience. However, the first attempt was so successful that I became 'barber elect' and was unable to refuse any member of the ship's company. Notice that I did not say "crew" because to merchant navy personnel the crew usually means the "ABs." The ship's officers dined in the saloon and the others grouped in mess rooms according to their lines of work and duties. All I can say is that without any preferential treatment everyone on board was soon sporting the hair cut of an officer.

Only the officers have uniforms with gold braid designating their status and occupation. Passenger ships could include the Purser and some administrators. The vast majority of merchant seamen had only civilian clothing but wore the exclusive silver **"MN"** lapel badge as their uniform in war. This was all that distinguished them during the war from non participants. This badge emblem is shown at the front of my book.

The *mv. Daghestan'* was owned by Messrs Common Bros. and they were one of the largest operators of merchant shipping. We were in time honoured fashion "tramping" on this trip. This meant heading for Adelaide with our cargo and our agents there would be endeavouring to find us another cargo for another destination which could be anywhere world wide. Thus we would freely load and unload according to demands and availability of goods determined by the local agents.

Departing the tropics I was susceptible to cooler climes. Temperatures dropped almost to sixty degrees Fahrenheit and although I had no complaints, nevertheless, I had to warm the sheets of my bunk by ironing them with my flat iron. Then, cosseted with five blankets, I would reach a modicum of comfort and fall asleep. These were the delights of abandoning the Red Sea but discomforts of the tropics still haunted me. In Adelaide I was enjoying dancing with a delightful partner until I was just beginning to break out into a sweat. Then it happened: torture, pain, irritation. I had to dash outside and strip off my shirt to cool down as "prickly heat" broke out. This was a frequent penalty of the Red Sea run and taken for granted with the high temperatures and profuse sweating. I had to admit it was suffered without mention as part of the course, but in Adelaide I was completely caught out with this surprise reminder which, if anything, was suddenly more intense and more irritating. It takes a bit of explaining to an unsuspecting partner who wonders what next will be shed? The obvious sudden distress signals I believe were the reassurances that I was not about to indulge in   spontaneous advances which were to say the least hardly subtle.

ADELAIDE

Adelaide was a pleasant little town with single storied houses well spread out on a relatively flat landscape. There were lots of green park areas and horse riding was a popular pastime which fitted in well with the terrain. I took a bus ride out to Broken Hill, an attractive creek with a waterfall tumbling throughout its length. This was the popular venue for families at the week end and presented an interesting view of local life. Shops in Adelaide were small and coupons were required for clothing, whilst coal was virtually non-existent. Train services, dependent upon coal, were minimal and even the radio station transmitted for a few hours only each day. Tobacco was rationed and the penalties of war had obviously imposed such restrictions. Food, fortunately, was freely available so I was able to sink my teeth into a particularly juicy steak. My skeletal frame was gaining weight at the rate of one pound per week since leaving Bombay and that curried menu. It was hardly surprising that I found a new lease of life and felt fitter than I had done for many months.

Strikes in Adelaide and probably throughout Australia, were sporadic and instituted on whims such as "It is raining" or, "The Grand National." Such an occasion provided sufficient excuse to refuse to work on the Saturday so that workers could attend the race. Our stay was extended a few days by strikes but I was not unhappy because we had more time in port. Even so, two weeks later we were again on our way, the destination Singapore.

SINGAPORE

Singapore was created from a swampy island and by 1823 Sir Stamford Raffles had laid the foundations of the city. He was a great believer in the British Empire and he established Singapore as a free port, a status which was zealously guarded. The Raffles Hotel was opened in 1899 and reflects the influence which he had in the region. It was interesting to view these outstanding buildings and to learn about their beginnings.

It was February 1941 when the Japanese inflicted the greatest ever defeat of the British as we unconditionally surrendered Singapore. Thence some would say prematurely. Closely following the end of War Two I arrived in Singapore and found it desperately run down. There was poverty, food shortages, unemployment and unrest. Open drainage in the form of three feet deep gutters on either side of roads revealed conditions that were hardly salubrious. Transport was available in the form of rickshaws and bicycles with sidecars. A very strong Chinese influence as well as Malayan meant I was experiencing other cultures and despite everything this visit was most interesting and enjoyable. Entertainment, not surprisingly, was lacking on this island of austerity.

MALAYSIA.

One third of our cargo, mainly flour, was discharged in Singapore thence we proceeded to Port Swettenham to unload some more. It was a short sail up the coast to this small port where rubber products were everywhere. Probably every member of the ship could be seen wearing some form of rubber footwear since it was relatively inexpensive. Pleasant excursions ashore each afternoon included perambulations which provided useful exercise but again the absence of shops and entertainment detracted from our enjoyment. I suppose it was to be expected that we would leave these rubber plantations and simply bounce up the coast. This we did and landed at Penang.

PENANG is an island with a reputation for fine beaches but the monsoon started and curtailed the pleasures of shore leave. Captain Francis Light of the East India Company in 1786 helped to establish the area from jungle. His son is credited as the founder of Adelaide so the 'Lights' were obviously considerable pioneers of some importance. My short explorations on bicycle rickshaws uncovered the real Chinatown atmosphere. Mosques and temples were numerous but weather and time left little opportunity for exploration.

Leaving Penang, **Piracy** was the problem which could not be ignored. The Straits of Malacca are infamous and historically were much feared in the days of sail. The light winds in the straits meant that ships under sail proceeded slowly and could easily be overtaken by the Malayan boats which were long, light and of shallow draught, so they were fast. Consequently, ships were overtaken, boarded and plundered. Tales of piracy were rife as we ourselves set off but our fears centred on speed boats and machine guns which were to be expected and posed a positive threat. We did not have a valuable cargo which was a blessing because ships were carefully scrutinised beforehand to ensure that there would be a prize haul. Nevertheless we were watchful for any craft which might come too close for comfort and enable pirates to board us.

Other captains, we understood, had been held at gun point whilst they were robbed and the ship rifled. In preparation of our defence we discussed the likelihood of an attack and formulated schemes to deal with every eventuality to protect ourselves. I was warned that as Radio Communicator I would be especially targeted and first to be silenced!

Looking back on those times nothing much has changed, except that the piracy is now even better planned and large ships have been disappearing either by being sunk or later re-appearing with a different identity and name. Whole cargoes have been stolen and sometimes all the crews were killed but on other occasions they could be spared to help run the ship under duress. Incidents happen every year and the menace remains real because, unfortunately, international co-operation is inadequate to put an end to twentieth century piracy. As I finalise these memoirs in 1997 this year resulted in 229 reported incidents with 51 seafarers having been killed.

On the subject of fighting, alcohol often was the precursor. On arrival back in Australia one peaceful Sunday evening, trouble broke out in the fo'c'sle as two sailors set about decorating each other's face. The brawl ended when the police were summoned with one fellow having blood dripping from a gaping bottle wound in his face. His forehead had a nasty gash and his ear was hanging off and bleeding profusely. The culprit who wielded the bottle was himself somewhat battered and he was marched off to spend six months in the cooler for assault. The victim went off to hospital to have parts more firmly attached and to stitch his ghastly wounds. We took on two new arrivals as replacements and at least peace then reigned up for'ard. Even without alcoholic stimulation there were always those individuals who thought that they could handle themselves and usually were victors of frequent skirmishes ashore. However, as with the boxing fraternity, no champion continues to win every fight. Unfortunately the thugs ashore do not fight under Queensberry Rules and there are no holds barred.

I recall a young lad of eighteen years of age when he went ashore in Egypt. He became involved in a brawl which resulted in his receiving a beating. The punishment must have included kicking because he was left the most pathetic mess from fisticuffs I ever witnessed. His face was so swollen that it looked like a swede turnip. It was purple, round and horribly misshapen. On closer inspection one could see where his eyes might be under two small slits from which sight was not possible. His teeth had come through his upper lip and it required stitches to pull the fragments of lip together. Few of his teeth were still present and those that did remain were precariously loose. His hearing was impaired and likely to be permanently damaged. Also his cheek bones would require surgery. His mouth could not function and he could neither speak nor eat. Liquid nourishment was fed using a spouted vessel or tube and a period in hospital care was required to help him back to our world. I wonder if ever he learned what I have gained from these experiences.

If one has to do battle, then do so with brains and not brawn.

FREEMANTLE & PERTH

Our orders were to proceed to Freemantle to load general cargo which in effect would mean collecting part cargo from various ports of call until our full complement was reached. Freemantle, Perth's port, is twelve miles down river at the mouth of the River Swan where Captain Freemantle of the British Navy landed in 1829.

The port was a small work-a-day town and with its old square model cars it seemed well behind the times. Of course since all vehicles then had to be imported from distant manufacturers these added costs made motor cars expensive items. Most were second hand old bangers which backfired and blew steam out of overheated radiators. Motor bikes were a less expensive substitute. The climate was ideally suited to this form of transport so that bikes almost outnumbered the cars.

PERTH

I took a trip into Perth, the capital of Western Australia. The town was forty-five minutes by road from Freemantle. The bus journey along a well-designed motorway revealed the most delightful scenery. I was very impressed with Perth which is situated on a beautiful stretch of the River Swan where it spreads out to a width of four miles to form a lake. Yachts with a bone in their teeth were scudding across in lively style in a stiff breeze and I was entranced with the exhilaration of the spectacle. The weather was splendid with soft puffy white cumulus clouds rolling across a brilliant blue sky. Aboard a yacht, enjoying this brisk breeze, must surely be the foretaste of paradise. Stricken by this rising wave of sea fever and under its spell this scene was truly bewitching.

The overall spaciousness of the lake almost in the centre of Perth, coupled with the spectacular scenery and splendid sailing certainly took my fancy. Neat, individually designed bungalows, nestled in the fresh spring growth with King's Park gardens and similar names all reminiscent of places back home. It captured my imagination so that I believed that this was the finest spot I had so far encountered. Perhaps I had to admit that it was more beautiful than Perth, Scotland, but despite all its attractions my strong homing instincts saved me from making a promise to settle here.
The climate was ideal and I gathered that Perth even had its own thermostat, a breeze known as the Freemantle Doctor. This regularly wafts in from the ocean on hot summer afternoons to cool the city and its beautiful beaches strung along the shore. What this breeze does to enliven sailing I can readily visualise. I doubted if any imaginary tropical island could compete with this heavenly combination of scenery and sailing. It is hardly surprising that several of our crew jumped ship and we were obliged to seek replacements.

The Australians were not unduly concerned so long as these new arrivals were British. Many young fellows thought that the austerity and rationing back in Britain would be less attractive than this land of opportunity. Consequently, some ships left with barely enough hands to take the ship on its way.

We had a pleasant sail round from Freemantle calling at **Wallaroo** for medical clearance before proceeding up to **Whyalla**. Both these places are up the Spencer Gulf near to Adelaide. We dropped anchor at Wallaroo and the following morning the doctor came out to issue our clearance certificate of good health. I guess he was new to the job and the sea was choppy for his small boat. By the time he arrived and clambered on board he was incapacitated by 'mal de mere.' No, I mislead my reader because he was sick, mighty sick as only seasickness can achieve. For the next couple of hours medical science failed him as he was flaked out believing he was dying or wishing he were dead whilst experiencing these two stages of seasickness.

Eventually we all filed into his room where a body in a chair groped for a pulse beat and if something was found ticking then another had passed his examination for freedom of infectious diseases. He was scarcely able to write up the necessary forms but with some assistance he at least managed to apply his signature. It was a safe bet that he felt he had earned his fee for that particular day and a fair bet that he was unlikely to pursue that branch of medicine.

Whyalla was a small port which had grown from its industrial beginnings of iron works and shipbuilding. The single cinema was open air style and presumably the expense of having it roofed over was unwarranted. At the time of year of our visit, additional clothing was necessary as some of our chaps had to vacate the cinema through feeling too cold. A ball was held at the week-end and if we were out in the 'bush' then we sure set it on fire. I think the 'Sheilas' encouraged us and I would suggest that they were no "two-pot screamers" (someone who cannot hold their drink). It was a ripper of a night and we followed it up with a few days fraternising with our newly acquired Aussie friends. Meanwhile, we were loading pig-iron into the lower parts of the ship as the first part of our cargo and then we headed for Melbourne.

MELBOURNE
Arriving in Melbourne we found that it was strike-bound and had

been without buses, trains or any form of transport over the preceding three weeks. Fortunately, we had a town berth and within twenty minutes we could walk into the centre of Melbourne. As a town it was uninspiring, altogether flat, though nicely positioned on the Yarra River. Numerous parks and wide thoroughfares did not endear it to me having already experienced the greater attractions of Perth. Nevertheless, the Victorian gold rush had left richly endowed public buildings and magnificent mansions built by wealthy merchants. It is Australia's second city and with its tramcars running along Elizabeth Street, the shops in Collins Street or gazing down Bourke Street towards Parliament House, one was impressed by a city that had been well planned. The Merchant Navy Flying Angel Seamen's Club which appears in many seaports world wide was particulary friendly and provided respite for tired limbs.

Outside the city, the road to Olinda twines upward through lovely woodland, then plunges into a eucalyptus forest and at times clings to the side of a mountain spur. It is only thirty miles from Melbourne and unless the visitor ventures to these Dandenong Ranges two thousand feet above sea level, it would be a serious oversight because the vistas in their sweep and colour are quite breathtaking. Likewise, the sardonic laughter of the kookaburra mingling with bird song, in a melodious bush symphony, is one of the delights of this Australian experience. I was only permitted to peep at the possibilities because Australia is astoundingly vast and our coastal trading seemed only to salt a prospective meal of extensive adventure.

SYDNEY

Another sprinkling of salt was added as we tasted Sydney, our next port of call. The harbour must be vying to be one of the very best in the world. The majestic curve of its harbour bridge forms an astonishing welcome to visitors arriving by sea. When it was completed in 1932 it was the largest arch bridge in the world. The main bridge consists of a steel arch span of 1,650 feet. The highest point 440 feet above sea level and the clearance for shipping is 170 feet at high water. The Captain Cook graving dock can accommodate an 80,000 ton liner for complete overhaul.

Across the expanse of choppy seas, within its magnificent harbour, an excitement of sleek yachts leaned their tall masts over as billowing white sails harnessed the fresh breeze in a lively display of nautical exuberance. Darting between the graceful craft, speeding motor boats criss-crossed the harbour with their plumes of irradiated white spindrift illuminated in the dazzling bright sunshine. Such a vision distils the true essence of the spell of the sea. The harbour sets the scene of these leisurely pursuits and the surrounding area extends to lots more sun, surf and sea as I realised when I dropped in at Bondi Beach. This has an Aussie ring to it and is a fine emblem of Sydney, forming my conclusion that Australia offered the greatest haven for water sports and outdoor activities that I had ever seen.

It was our good fortune to have the Australian strikes delay our loading for several days. In Melbourne our six day visit was extended to nineteen days and in Sydney what could have been achieved in two days was extended to one week. Sydney exceeded all expectations and having experienced other Australian towns I was not prepared for a fashionable down town centre of arcades and department stores with pedestrian congestion equalling the Saturday night proportions of a city. What was lacking was style and I shopped for shoes with pointed toes or even brogue designs but could only find versions of square ludicrous primitive shapes. I was also astounded that the male population wore full black suits complete with a collar and tie, whereas most of us popped about in shirt sleeves or shorts. Possibly it was conventional business wear but sensibly the ladies wore print frocks and flimsy summer dresses which naturally we flattered with our attention. One lady was arrested, however, for shopping in a scanty bathing suit. This was surprising since topless bathing is common and they even had official nudist beaches. Australia is indeed a country of contrasts extending from this jostling seafaring city to the deserted dust dry outback. That it is the largest island in the world is demonstrated by the great distances between places and the vast changes in both climate and terrain.

Cricket seemed to be an obsession because in the shop windows there was continuous television showing the English touring team at play. The game could also be followed on a gigantic green board erected in the city square. The ball and play, possibly magnetically operated, could be studied as the test matches proceeded. Needless to say, any sight of the game drew considerable crowds on each pavement as they peered into the shop windows to follow the progress of the match with an enthusiasm that was quite amazing.

BRISBANE

Brisbane was our final port of call. The climate was sub tropical and it has its status as the holiday state of Australia. Historically, it began as a penal settlement and there were bloody battles with the Aborigines. Somehow these facts seemed to linger and my quick impression was that the residents formed a more stubborn group. I attended the England versus Australia Test Match 1946. Watching the cricket, I was seated on a grass banking in brilliant sunshine having a most enjoyable afternoon, following the play, when along came a hulking great bush whacker wearing his wide brimmed Aussie hat. He sat down immediately in front of me entirely blocking my view with shoulders wide enough to obliterate the entire cricket pitch. I could not move to left or right because I was in a row of similarly seated spectators. After a minute or two, struggling to catch a glimpse of the play, I tapped this fellow on the shoulder and asked politely if he could possibly move slightly to his left or right, where nobody was seated, so that I could see. He turned and looked at whatever was wriggling in the grass behind him and his veiled threat suggested, "Huh!" He neither spoke nor moved and it seemed probable that had he received another request he would have with one slow movement of his great hand extinguished the irritant with as little concern as swatting a fly.

I moved away having lost my vantage point where I had enjoyed a good afternoon of cricket until that disappointment. One cannot criticise the whole country over one incident but it confirmed my opinion that the Australians are a physical people, forthright and unnerving if one expects English manners.

I ventured to an area of swamps and creeks which was crocodile territory. Large crocs I avoided but from newt size to a couple of feet long I was happy to hold them playfully with the element of risk adding to the excitement. A carved crocodile by an aborigine was my selected souvenir for this interesting excursion.

CHINESE WATERS & PACIFIC OCEAN
Leaving Brisbane we headed for Hong Kong with a strange and suspicious character on board. He had been accepted by our agents and imposed upon us as our only passenger. Normally we did not take passengers so this chappie must have been influential. Mr. Lee was in fact a tall elegant Englishman who had spent many years in China, hence our referring to him as 'Ching Lee.' The captain was highly suspicious of him in view of our sailing area and its association with piracy. The last thing the captain wanted was a saboteur actually on his ship. Nobody knew the source of Mr. Lee's wealth or the nature of his business and our anxiety would have soared had we known the purpose of his silver topped cane. This he carried frequently and when stepping ashore, it was part of his attire, as an Englishman would, in London, have carried his rolled umbrella.

The discovery unfolded on the first night ashore when an uncomfortable situation developed in a seedy part of town. One of our group must have foolishly stepped out of line to occasion great anger and it seemed that we might be set upon. Ching Lee turned the silver knob of his walking stick and withdrew a gleaming sword. The elegant cane was actually a sword stick and he wielded it like 'Steed' in the Avengers. He uttered a great string of suggestions

200

in Cantonese which astonished us and confounded the Chinese. There was no more trouble, other than a lecture later, on how to behave according to Ching Lee.

HONG KONG

First impressions of *Hong Kong* were of course the waterborne craft in the form of the famous Chinese Junks with their fully battened junk rigged sails. Like many Arab Dhows they also carried the familiar 'thunder box' projecting from the stern rail. This is the Eastern equivalent of what our older sailing ships had up forward of the fo'c'stle from cathead to cathead and known as the beakhead. The gratings which formed the deck was used by the crew as their lavatory. Hence our nautical reference to the lavatory as the "heads." I studied these magical Chinese craft which frequently bore an eye painted on their bow to ward off evil spirits. I was fascinated to see the small cannons mounted on numerous junks. These were proper gunpowder operated weapons for defence against piracy in these waters. Better equipped junks had machine guns. Boats are constantly being raided and captains of small coastal craft have to pay protection money or suffer the consequencies. My attention to these junks was only distracted by the congestion of small sampans on which so many of the population live and trade. Hong Kong is an island and it has the busiest deepwater harbour in the world. It was seized by the British in 1841 and this British territory sadly will be returned to China in 1997.

Immediately I saw the island, rising steeply like a mountain out of the bay, I knew that I must climb to its peak. Victoria Peak was reached by a funicular railway and its amazing ride to the top offered magnificent scenery with the final views from the peak absolutely spectacular. The freshness on top contrasted sharply with the intensive living and congestion in the narrow streets of the town down below. Obviously, the well-to-do choose to live in these loftier parts, where a pleasant walk on a pathway around the top of the island, offers glorious views of the bay.

I had heard that if anything goes missing from the ship, a type-writer for example, one should hasten immediately to "Thief Street" and the likelihood would be that it would be found being presented for sale. Certainly, the marketing in that street is quite amazing and reminiscent of Glasgow Barrowland but of course Chinese style. Apart from the enormous variety of goods offered for sale, more astonishing perhaps was the range of food on display: Fine species of beetles were roasted to perfection. Sugared cockroaches were all pleasantly presented in large baskets. Whole roasted pigs were available complete with whiskers and tails which reminded one in no uncertain terms of the meat source.

Other products were hen intestines which had been crisped or even rats if rodents were preferred. The disappearance of both of our cats was easily explained as no other ship left port with its moggie. The meat was said to be very tasty but perhaps it was being compared with bird nest pie or shark fin soup. From duck feet to cockerels' combs the variety of nutrients amazed me, though it has to be said that I strictly limited my gastronic impulses. Chinese cooking Western fashion remains my preference as there seemed to be absolutely nothing absent from true Chinese preparations. On the other hand, perhaps it was just the honesty of the presentation that left nothing to the imagination which I found somewhat offensive.

Chinese dentistry also claimed my attention when I heard the loud beating of drums and clashing cymbals used to attract the attention of prospective clients. Possibly, the din also submerged the screams of those being treated and took the patient's mind off the operation. In the midst of a crowded street, the victim sat on a chair whilst the dentist, without recourse to anesthetic or even a whiff of cocaine, was extracting offending teeth. He seemed to prise out the teeth using an instrument like a screwdriver as a lever. When one extraction became difficult he resorted to what I regarded suspiciously as pliers. At the most excruciating moment the drums and cymbals were increased to full volume so that I couldn't hear any of the screaming. The patients could not be said to be enjoying their spell in the dentist's chair but there was no shortage of volunteers. A couple of ten year old children survived the ordeal without much flinching. I mean there was nobody holding them down on the chair. Once the extraction was completed a piece of rolled paper was inserted into the hole created and the patient's mouth firmly clamped tightly shut as he was instructed to bite hard on the paper plug to stop the bleeding. Needless to say, it was difficult for the patient to scream or he would lose the paper plug and so silence reigned. I was curious to find out how painful the extractions were but I did not volunteer as I didn't think my teeth were that bad!

When I returned to the UK. I described the primitive implements I had seen in these operations to my local dentist. He was not altogether surprised because in our early days of dentistry similar instruments had been employed professionally, until recently superseded by more sophisticated apparatus. Thus it seems that I had not been witnessing extractions facilitated by anything as gruesome as a tacklifter or a screwdriver. Even so I still preferred my dentist's cocaine to those cymbals.

I was fascinated with the Chinese skills of intricate carving in wood or ivory and ranging from large camphor wood chests to minuscule jewelry. The extraordinary care and patience required to fashion these items together with the countless hours of work involved was quite amazing. Thus my souvenirs were representative of these skills and I still enjoy them as I reflect upon my unique memories of Hong Kong.

The aspect of Hong Kong life which I didn't like was the degree of subjugation of the women. When luggage was carried ashore it was by women. Considered to be the inferior sex, hard work and menial jobs were apportioned to them. Our ship was swarming with women doing the washing up for our cook and cleaning for the stewards. Washy washy or sew sew girls took on our laundry or repairs washing and darning. They were rewarded with hard loaves, sugar or something from the pantry. I was "sweet" on one young girl, a shop assistant, and since we were getting along splendidly I tried to fix a date outside her working hours. This proved difficult as she worked from 8am till 8pm seven days per week. This fact I could verify and it rather moderated any courting.

SHANGHAI
Further experience of Chinese culture was gained when we travelled on to Shanghai which was the largest City in China. The impressive waterfront, along the great Yangtze Kiang River, was known as the Bund. I still have in my office a framed picture in silk of this amazing river front with the magnificent buildings which seem quite European but are viewed across the mighty river teeming with its sampans and junks. Ashore, the atmosphere is distinctly Chinese and despite the Bund being the best known street in the Orient, material poverty and a frenetic life style dominated. Even more of the population seemed to live on board water borne craft and the river was almost as congested as life ashore. Food was too expensive for us to partake in hotels or restaurants and generally the length of time spent ashore was determined by one's appetite. The weather was cold as it was early January, 1947, but this allowed some of our enterprising crew to sell off their pullovers and clothing at great profit, in a changey changey trading racket. When we left Shanghai colleagues were reduced almost to underwear having sold all their gear for a tempting profit. Likewise, everyone was cleaned out of cigarettes which fetched good prices. These business deals quite reversed the normal flow of goods but this was due to the high costs of living in Shanghai.

PACIFIC OCEAN
We sailed out on to the Pacific Ocean and headed for Vancouver, anticipating following seas and fair winds, but the exact opposite ensued and this was extraordinary for the season. The weather

changed ominously as a typhoon was forecast. Suddenly, the barometer dropped dramatically and within minutes a swell built up from moderate, increasing rapidly until it exceeded forty feet. These waves rolled towards us and continued to increase so that even within the first hour they became mountainous. From a bright calm day the heavens blackened and seemed to drop down over us until it was almost dark. The wind quickly responded as it doubled in strength and immediately reached hurricane force before one realised what was happening. Torrents of rain were hurled over the ship, striking the superstructure with the stinging force of solid buckshot. The howls of the wind shrieked with ear splitting intensity and each halliard and stay on the ship vibrated until they wailed like banshees. The whole ship shuddered as it crashed forward, plunging into walls of oncoming sea which now towered well above the height of our bridge. What was so amazing was the speed with which it increased and the fierceness and intensity of the typhoon as all the forces overwhelmed us in a dark foreboding shroud.

I was not able to venture out on to the open wings of the bridge as the stinging rain engulfed me and the violence of the wind almost tore the flesh off my face. The sea was a mass of white crests with spume and spray being driven horizontally across the ocean. The ship was completely shrouded in wind, rain and sea, so that visibility was zero. Ahead nothing could be seen. We were enveloped in the terror of the tyhoon. In Chinese "tai fung" means "big wind" and there is little wonder that Chinese sailors treat typhoons with the utmost respect. They run for cover at the first hint of trouble yet many still are lost by the great power of this phenomenal hazard.

Suddenly, almost in minutes, the wind dropped and the typhoon blew itself out as it neared the coast well behind us. We were left to recover as it rapidly filled and died. The change was remarkable, like entering a new world. The storm ceased, the skies cleared and the seas flattened to a confused swell. The motion of the ship eased to a rhythmic roll again, which was heavy but tolerable, being tamed from the wild fury of the typhoon. At its height the storm lasted for only a few hours, although at one stage we rolled violently, shipping more seas than desired. Damage was limited as we turned at that point and headed into the wind. The rolling at that point had become too dangerous. One particular sea almost rolled us over and we were obliged to change course to allay the threat from those mountainous seas.

Possibly at the back of one's mind was the fact that our ship's licence was due for renewal and a major overhaul was required. It was not the best time to test the ship with the grey widow-maker.

We continued, but it was uncomfortable and wet with persistant westerly winds impeding our progress. Several knots were knocked off our speed which was much reduced as we crashed headlong into buffeting seas. The result was a tedious extended passage traversing this vast ocean. Normally after two weeks at sea all minds are focussed on shore leave. Prospects of the new port are discussed and thirsts are stimulated because most tramp steamers are "dry" and thoughts on the pleasures of a run ashore are a psychological balm.

We were battling forward into these seas and our progress was monotonously slow, so that irritabilities surfaced through frustration and knowing that there was no possibility of making a landfall for well over another week. Tempers were fraying and an atmosphere of mistrust was building up amongst the crew. There were accusations of theft and suggestions of interference with each other's private property. The cook in particular was claiming that someone had messed about with his pans and equipment and had even pinched some of his preparations. Retaliation was to accuse him of growing idle and too weary to produce decent food.

Superstitions permeated the ship and even demons and ghosts became topics of conversation. Fears mounted with some believing that we might become another "Marie Celeste" and our ship would be found mysteriously abandoned as it drifted alone out on the ocean. It is hard to imagine that a few weeks of isolation from land could engender such spiritual exaggerations. But we were a tiresome ship, alone and bobbing about in mid ocean, with our progress rated at a walking pace. It was still thousands of miles to reach land and apparently there was little likelihood of our situation altering for many days. Instead of leadership or stiff reprimands to stifle these complaints, the confrontations were becoming more intense and more numerous.

Something serious was going to happen because ghostly sightings at night were vociferously touted, though suggestions of spectres robbing folks was not accepted as an excuse even on this haunted ship. Murder and knifing attacks threatened forebodingly as whispering campaigns hustled antagonists together in opposing groups.

Disaster was inevitable and soon festering forces dealt the fearful blow. I saw the bosun mounting the steps to the bridge and I heard him telling the Third Mate that a member of the crew had gone missing. Apparently George had been ordered to paint the stern rails of the ship. He was last seen painting peacefully, but now he could not be found and his paint brush was left lying on the deck but there was no sign of George. Almost an hour had elapsed since he was last seen. The captain was called and he examined the facts. He discounted any suggestions that mysterious forces had overwhelmed him. He did not dwell on the claims of murder. It was not dangerous to be painting the rails of the ship. Nevertheless, it was possible that George could have overreached, lost his balance and fallen overboard. Others declared that he had been overcome by looming suicidal pressures and that threatening thoughts had built up sufficiently to disturb him and cause him to jump overboard.

The ship's position was carefully noted on the chart, before turning about and sailing back along our reciprocal course. Lookouts were stationed throughout the ship and there were many anxious eyes peering in every direction as we retraced our tract. We searched with concentration and care, all eyes engaged on the task. Binoculars were used to improve the distance that could be scanned. Despite these best endeavours no trace of George was found. Comprehension of the Pacific Ocean when viewed in these circumstances is seen to be vast, lonely and cruel. Even though the situation seemed hopeless every effort was made to retrieve any signs of George until finally the conclusion was reached that he had disappeared and drowned. Perhaps we could wish that he might go aloft and reach Fiddler's Green.

 The nervousness on board was now intense with fraying tempers and fear in every glance. It was therefore with alarm, I witnessed the next incident, when I spotted our bosun. He was visibly shaken and agitated as he remonstrated with the carpenter for not properly securing the hatch cover. Tempers were flaring and the insults which were sparked off seemed about to fire real trouble till the 2nd Mate intervened. He saw the inadequately fastened hatch cover and wrenched it open to behold with amazement that there were six stowaways hiding down in the hold of the ship. This at last was the explanation for all these mysterious sightings and the numerous thefts, as they came out at night and stole food to survive. Soon extra paintbrushes were organised for them as they were set to work, chipping and painting, in return for their accommodation. Needless to say, tempers simmered down as imagined sightings were now accepted as having been factual, however fanciful the accounts may have at first seemed.

DIRECTION FINDING
We were still rolling very heavily with crockery and plates being smashed daily. The weather continued thick and overcast. There was little wonder that the captain looked apprehensive as we headed inwards towards the coast, hampered by constant poor visibility. It was a frightening thought that we did not know how far off the coast we might be and if he had underestimated our progress then, at any moment, we might feel a crunch as we struck

and pounded on the rocks of an off lying shoal. Unless something became visible soon or the weather improved, the next twenty-four hours would be a nerve-wracking experience. Little wonder the captain seemed worried and he would become even more agitated until our position could be determined accurately.

Eventually the captain approached me and asked if I could possibly pick up some signals on my Direction Finding equipment. As neither he nor the 2nd Mate could say within a few hundred miles where we were. Our position was calculated simply by dead reckoning and this had been confused through sailing back to search for George. Poor visibility had ruled out position finding by sextant as neither the sun nor stars had been visible for weeks. Strong head winds had affected our speed and the effects of the typhoon made calculations for leeway very difficult. Altogether, our position on the chart was pure guesswork as apart from the ship's log and compass no other instruments were available. Furthermore, we had been four weeks at sea and small errors are multiplied by the number of hours involved.

I searched with my Direction Finder for likely Radio Beacons and was able to pick up faint signals from one source. I announced our bearing and position line from that beacon explaining that we must be some five hundred miles distant because of the weakness of the signal and the absence of other radio beacons. The captain was much relieved with this information because it meant that at least we were not about to crash into the coast. Also, it coincided with a good estimate of our possible position.

Several hours later I gave the captain an updated plot which I had been able to determine because I had picked out another radio beacon and the bearings from these two beacons crossed to pin point our position. The captain was delighted because again it confirmed the plot was along my previous position line. To bring a fully laden ship to a sudden halt, even with engines full astern, requires over a mile of sea room. There are no brakes that can be operated to stop a ship. It is therefore necessary to know what lies, almost an hour, ahead if one is to proceed safely or one must reduce speed drastically.

My task now was continuous and at hourly intervals I passed my findings to update our position so that we could proceed in safety. Repeatedly, there was a consistency with my calculations and a trail of crosses was drawn on our chart as we headed towards Vancouver.

Later I was able to pick up signals from a third beacon which capitalised on my previous work. Drawing position lines from three beacons determines a more accurate plot. In theory these three lines would meet at one spot but usually it results in a small triangle known as the 'cocked hat.' The smaller this triangle the more accurate the determined position. My position findings virtually met at one spot and my repeated reports left little doubt about the exact position of the ship.

It was natural that the captain had viewed Direction Finding as a new fangled and a mysterious piece of unreliable equipment. His previous experiences possibly had affirmed this opinion and he regarded it as almost worthless. This was not surprising because of the number of errors that could occur. Obviously, three bearings have to be determined as near instantaneously as possible to obtain the accurate cross. Each bearing requires calculations to be made, involving simultaneous reporting of the ship's heading by compass, which is then compared with the direction finder bearing of each radio beacon. Errors in the system have to be applied before arriving at the final figures. The skill of the radio operator is paramount in determining the outcome.

When the beacon is heard a coil is turned until the signal strength fades to zero. That is the theory but invariably the signal dies out as the coil is turned and then turning it further the signal reappears again as it becomes audible. The skill is determining between these two audible points, within the silent interval, where the centre of zero sound is located. This can extend perhaps to ten degrees so that there is ample room for error and a number of mathematical calculations are involved allowing for errors by ship's magnetism and the ship's compass. A simple analogy is revolving a portable domestic radio and finding the variation in strength of the broadcast sound. My equipment was of course more sophisticated and our performance now was encouraging. As we closed the coast I was reporting our position hourly and as the signal strength improved this facilitated determination of the bearings because the silent interval narrowed.

It was midnight and not the most opportune time to enter a strange port. The captain decided because of the fog and in the darkness of night, it would be sensible to turn about and sail back on our reciprocal course for two hours. Then at dawn we would head back inwards towards Vancouver, hoping that the visibility might have improved.

I had been constantly engaged in calculations and direction finding during the previous thirty-six hours and was relieved to hear that I could now go and catch two hours sleep. Wearily, I heard my recall at four am. and I tuned in to the three radio beacons to ascertain our latest position. I reported my findings to the First Mate but he just laughed and said, "It's all right, Sparks, but you are still asleep! I have seen the light and know where we are now so for once you have slipped up." I quickly checked my bearings and determined our position yet again. "It is you who are wrong," I said with emphasis. "This position I insist is accurate." The first mate charged out on to the wing of the bridge and checked the light to which he was heading. It was "Frying Pan Shoal!" Those rocks would have ripped us to pieces.

Rapidly he corrected the ship's course, thus averting certain disaster. It is a well known failing to be watching carefully for a channel light and when a light does show up to heave a sigh of relief believing that the target has been located. He apologised to me and was profuse in his thanks for my endeavours. Later in the vicinity of Vancouver we hoisted the international code flag "G" indicating that we required a pilot. We picked up our pilot and flew the red and white flag "H," indicating "we have a pilot on board." We docked safely and were soon over run with custom officers searching the ship with particular diligence since we hailed from China.

I overheard the captain talking to the pilot and describing to him the most remarkable display of direction finding he had ever witnessed. He was well pleased with our achievement having been able to enter port in poor visibility after weeks at sea and without recourse to the sextant. That was ruled out because of fog, sleet and blizzards in the last two weeks of our passage. Noon sightings of the sun or finding stars at night had been impossible. The D.F. had come into its own and I felt vindicated and pleasantly satisfied with the accuracy of my earlier corrections to this equipment.

VANCOUVER

We had taken twenty-seven days to cross the Pacific and rolled like a pendulum most of the way. My reactions, apart from a western roll in my gait, were quite interesting. I visited the barber in Vancouver and whilst seated in his chair, I noticed that he placed his cup of coffee on the glass shelf. Immediately, I eased myself forward from the chair and put his cup down firmly beside his washbasin. "What the heck are you doing?" he enquired. I replied that his cup would fall off the shelf. At that moment, I suddenly realised that I was no longer on the ship and that the barber's shop would be unlikely to roll! My reactions were instinctive and induced through several weeks of constant rolling about at sea. We had lost so many cups and plates that each of us on board captured a cup and looked after it because otherwise we would have to await a cup being re-allocated.

Vancouver was stunningly beautiful in a setting of steep forested mountains rising up from the sea which entered several inlets making the area a coastal paradise. There was ample opportunity for sailing with water sports and excellent beaches as a bonus.

Vancouver is named after Captain George Vancouver who mapped this coast in 1792. I was delighted to find that the citizens were enormously proud of their Scottish forebears. Tartan garments and trimmings were displayed in the shops and widely worn. One shop in the high street had heather growing outside and it appeared that goods originating in Scotland meant that such items were sold as select. Genuine Scottish grain leather brogues were on display with sprigs of heather enhancing their attractions and displayed against a background of tartan and tweeds. The butcher had the slogan *We hae meat that Ye can eat* and even the barber found a *Burn's* quotation appropriate:

Oh wad some Power the giftie gie us
To see oursels as ithers see us!

Stanley Park which extends to 1,000 acres of natural rain forest is the city's favourite playground. Towering totem poles face Coal Harbor and it is an area of considerable interest for excursions. The Capilano Trading Post displays these authentic totem poles which have been restored and painted. One could discuss these native arts with an authentic Indian carver. Nearby is a 450 foot suspension bridge swaying 230 feet above the Capilano River. If you have a head for heights it is unnerving, but like myself, if you haven't then it was petrifying. The gaps between the planking were fully three inches wide and I had no doubt that if I didn't step carefully I would fall downwards between them and plummet into oblivion. The bridge sways with the slightest encouragement not always taken into account when someone charges on to it 300 feet away at the far end. The narrow rails of both sides of the bridge can just be spanned and held by both hands but even so palpitations race ahead of your thoughts as you gaze all the way down into the canyon and listen to the thundering roars of the Capilano River raging far below.

The adjacent mountains provide another popular playground. When I visited the Seamen's Mission I learned that a party would be led up the famous Grouse Mountain to see the Vancouver Third International Ski Championship. Thus on Sunday morning I arose at six am. and suitably reinforced with a supply of sandwiches, I set off to meet the party and make the climb. A bus took us up to the 800 ft. level and we then climbed through dense aromatic pine woods which were clinging to the steep mountain side. The path seemed to ascend vertically and after the first hour I realised that I was a seafarer unaccustomed to these shoreside pursuits. A further half hour of striving and I had reached an altitude of 2,000ft. but, having started, I convinced myself that I must finish even if the mind was willing but not receiving ample physical encouragement.

After climbing a further thousand feet, the snow line was reached, where the woods cleared to reveal the Georgia Lodge strategically perched for the weary and it looked really inviting. The log cabin served the most delectable blue-berry pie I had ever tasted. The berries were picked from surrounding bushes in the summertime. Perhaps it was the sharp crisp air or after such a rugged climb that I was enormously hungry but I voraciously demolished that pie.

Having momentarily halted the climbing, this respite had restored the blood flow to my aching limbs and the coursing gastric juices certainly appreciated that rapturous morsel. Then, still relishing thoughts of that blue-berry pie, I found new stamina to propel my legs into action again. I fastened spikes to my boots and tackled the hard carpet of snow, powering upwards to around 4,000ft. The ski-ing at the top was both novel and interesting but it was just too enticing to simply remain a mere observer so, without more ado, I launched into the ski-ing but not of course into the championship!

Realising that a Scottish accent was probably the answer to captivating feminine companionship, my diction generously vibrated with the rolling of "R's" wherever possible. Almost immediately a sympathetic spirit arose to become suitably entranced. This partnered stay of three weeks bonded on an ascending plain

214

until that painful time of parting. It can be a cruel world where inevitably one has to take one's leave and feel the pain of a warm relationship being brutally dashed in despair on the rocks of departure.

"The Leavin" is an event which every sailor experiences and it is a highly charged emotional time. He needn't be married or newly-wed, because most young sailors will have bonded to a beating heart ashore. *The Leavin* sequel which follows means sailing away out on to a lonely ocean and suffering with an emptiness which is prolonged, agonising and devastating. The young sailor drifting away from his new love will feel the pain and evanescence of his emotional relationship.

It can be heartrending enough when the scene is a departing train leaving the station with fond farewells fluttering in the waves of goodbye. However romantic the vanishing carriages might appear, it bears little of the emotionally charged atmosphere which a ship portrays as it majestically slips the quay to glide serenely out into the ocean. The severance is protracted as slowly, drowning in the sound of the ship's siren, two hearts are irrevocably torn apart. This is a heartbreaking experience where the moisture of damp eyes both ashore and afloat, best express life at its most poignant. Despite this suffering and view of the world, where farewells go out sighing, it is not what I imply as seeing the world through 'salt sprayed eyes' yet this too is involved. Everyone knows that 'all the nice girls love a sailor' and nice young sailors leaving port invariably are seeing the world through dampened eyes, at least figuratively speaking. My *"leavin* of Vancouver" was no exception. I did start to ponder, however, if I should settle down ashore somewhere. The hunter then could avoid being the haunted.

PANAMA CANAL
Another adventure was pending as we approached our passage through the Panama Canal. The Canal cuts across the Isthmus of Panama to link the Pacific and Atlantic Oceans. It is one of the

215

greatest engineering achievements in the world. When completed in 1914 the journey from San Francisco to New York was shortened to 5,200 miles(8370km) as opposed to rounding Cape Horn and South America over a distance of 13,000 miles(2091km). The Panama Canal is 81.63 kilometres long and we expected to proceed from the Pacific to the Atlantic in about eight to twelve hours. The narrowest point is 150 metres wide and the widest section is the 422 square kilometres of Gatun Lake. The direction of the canal as we were heading was from SE to NW.

Entering the canal from the Pacific first the Miraflores locks raise the ship in two chambers, the actual height depending upon the tide in the Pacific. Tides at the Pacific end rise about four metres but the Atlantic tides rise only sixty centimetres daily. Once out of the locks, Miraflores Lake a distance of two point four kilometres is crossed. The Pedro Miguel locks then follow and in one step the ship is raised nine metres. Electric locomotives pull the ship into the locks and when raised it sails into the Gaillard Cut which is one way traffic and thirteen kilometres long.

Leaving the Cut we sailed across Gatun Lake which is created by the Gatun Dam one of the greatest in the world. An 18-million cubic metre earth dam created Gatun Lake by holding back the waters of the Chagres River which flows into the Atlantic. Then in three steps we were lowered to the level of the Atlantic ocean by the Gatun Locks. Each lock took about ten minutes to negotiate and the locomotives or mules run on rails on both sides of the locks to help guide and pull the ship through each lock. The locks operate in pairs as it is two way traffic. The drop to the Atlantic is about twenty-six metres from Gatun Lake.

It is difficult to realise that yellow fever and malaria carrying mosquitos defeated all attempts to construct the canal as it was first dug out of the swamps. Thousands died of epidemics of tropical diseases and in 1882 Marie de Lessops who had previously directed the construction of the Suez Canal had to abandon the work as his enterprise went bankrupt. The United States then undertook its construction and the miraculous passage was completed. It carries on average about thirty-four ships per day.

Once more an open sea welcomed us and having crossed the Pacific Ocean and now venturing to cross the Atlantic the vastness of these two great oceans emphasised that seventy-one per cent of the world's surface area is water. The Pacific rates fifty per cent, the Atlantic twenty-five per cent and the Indian Ocean which we crossed earlier fifteen per cent. The remaining ten per cent is made up of the minor seas like the Mediterranean, Baltic, North Sea etc. It is hardly surprising that this amount of water has a stabilizing   effect upon our climate. It is reckoned that if the heat radiation from the sun increased its energy output by one per cent in the course of a year and if the heat all went into the atmosphere it would raise its temperature 15 degs.C.(27F). Some parts of the earth would become intolerably hot. But the same amount of heat would raise the temperature of the oceans by only 0.1degs.C.

The greatest height on land is Mount Everest 29,028 feet above sea level but the greatest depth of all oceans is the "Challenger Deep" 36,000 feet below sea level. Thinking about this from the point of view of the sea floor we, in fact, sail over peaks which are higher than mount Everest. Also if Mt.Everest were dropped into that deep trench we could still sail over it with a clearance of one mile depth. We also find below the surface of the sea mountain ranges higher than the Himalayas and gorges deeper than the Grand Canyon. The world under the sea is larger than our dry land and it remains a vast underwater frontier for exploration. If all the land were bulldozed into the sea it would be covered by water to a depth of 8,000 feet. The sea as always can pronounce on our   significance.

We were now eagerly awaiting a radio message with information on where to dock in the UK. to discharge our grain cargo. A sweepstake was being run with bets on the first port of call. I was being anxiously watched because I would be first to know but because of secrecy I could only divulge information of this kind to the captain. As we approached the UK. it was obvious that some excited individuals had already got the "Channels." They were packing and re-packing and internally in turmoil with thoughts of arriving home. If anyone should have been suffering this infamous "Channel Fever" on board this ship it should have been myself. It was well over two years since I had parted from these shores. First disappearing out East, rounding the world and to reappear returning from the West. Channel fever derives its name from seamen trying to describe the excitement on board ship created as the homeward destination is approached. The excitement and fever mounts the closer they reach shore leave and loved ones. The longer the voyage the greater the degree of fever.

Homeward-bounders dangled a rope-end over the ship's side for ' wives and sweethearts to pull the ship home.'

> *And it's haul away, girls, steady and true,*
> *Dolly and Molly, Polly and Sue,*
> *Mothers and sisters and sweethearts and all,*
> *Haul away, all the way, haul away, haul!*

13

FIRE AND FIRING SQUAD

BALTIC SEA

Home leave meant two months spent with family and friends as earned by over two years absence at sea. My folks were astounded at my yellow palor which was a combination of the time which I had spent in the tropics and "Mepacrine," the anti-malaria drug which I had been taking. My appearance contrasted sharply with the peaches and cream complexions of friends and family. My skin resembled dried parchment and I was uniquely sallow. Still duck yellow on the "Thirteenth" of June 1947 I signed articles for the **SS.CANFORD** at Hull. Whether the date proved lucky or unlucky will depend upon one's point of view. I faced death whilst a member of this ship and because I experienced these close encounters one might say that I was unlucky and that followed from the thirteenth. But I consider myself extremely lucky because here I am present to write about these events. It is rather how I view the proverbial bottle which I usually think of as being half full rather than half empty. The fact that I joined the ship on the thirteenth meant that I was committed and no longer had the option of a full bottle.

The ship was 2,000 Grt. and built by the Germans in 1944 but we confiscated her before she had sailed. The radio gear had been replaced by Marconi and I was pleased to see that we were fitted with the latest type of receiver and Direction Finder equipment.

Altogether she was a nice little Baltic Trader and we were bound for the Gulf of Bothnia in the Baltic Sea.

There was a minor hitch as we set off on our first trip. Just off Grimsby Roads the helmsman suggested that the ship didn't answer to the wheel. We then rammed a trawler at anchor so that certainly proved his point. We carried away her forward mast, stove in her midships and had to hover to see whether or not either of us would sink. I was kept busy on the radio, communicating these circumstances and co-ordinating help from ashore.

In due course we recovered from this situation and continued once more on our way. Some hours later the steering became unmanageable and would not respond to the helm. What about unlucky thirteen? In these circumstances it is better to concentrate on defeating the obstacles rather than bemoaning the facts.

We rigged up rope steering which was operated by our winches and we were able to crawl back into port. Repairs were carried out but nobody fully understood the whims of the German Electric steering system. Consequently, when were reached the same spot, off the coast, we again had problems. We grappled with the steering until we were able to operate it on a manual emergency system. This meant that the helmsman had to turn the wheel about sixteen turns to take us from hard starboard to hard over in the opposite direction. Apart from a tiring spell at the wheel our helmsman soon acquired the knack of keeping us out of further trouble for the moment.

Brunsbuttel is at the western end of the Kiel Canal and it was there that we got our ship "wiped." This replaced the previous system of degausing for protection against mines. Many still lurked about coastal waters and this was the method of thwarting the magnetic menace. The ship is passed over many coils of wire with a heavy current passing through them so that the ship is polarised. Having had to turn several times to pass over the coils, the steering gear became erratic. We anchored alongside in the canal to repair a burst oil pipe in the steering system and my attention became drawn to an attractive thatched house. On top was a bundle of straw which I inspected with the binoculars and saw that it was a stork complete with her family in the nest. This was the first stork I had seen and I was happy that it didn't foretell any family foibles that I could subsequently encounter. I still believed that there was little to fear from that signing on date.

KIEL CANAL

Kiel Canal offered a delightful passage with glorious sunshine and scenery. It is of course the short cut from the North Sea to the Baltic Sea. Brunsbuttelkoog is at the mouth of the Elbe River entering at the North Sea and then extending sixty-one miles to Holtenau at Kiel harbour on the Baltic Sea. The canal is 338 feet wide and 37 feet deep with seven high level bridges with heights of 140 feet. It was built 1887-1895 then enlarged for German naval ships in 1914. Since 1919, when it was nationalised, it has come under German administration.

All along the canal we passed bathers and sunbathers and many were stunning examples of our foreign species with some of the bodies being female. That I could see without the aid of binoculars but there was no harm in making sure! There was so much of interest to soak up with strips of land under various types of cultivation and some areas where peat was being dug. Peasants were stacking it to dry in the sun for fuel. On both banks a kaleidoscope of human activity constantly revealed much to interest and make this canal passage particularly enjoyable. There was also a variety of barges and boats using the canal and many that could stimulate a sailor to dream.

SWEDEN

Holmsund near Umea in Sweden was our destination for a cargo of timber. Pine forests surrounded us and down one side of the river logs chained together formed the passageway for floating timber downstream. From the upper reaches of the Fjord log shutes fed the flow of logs into the current. The air was crisp and fresh and in the damp atmosphere the pine woods released their wonderful perfume. Seldom could sailors find themselves anchored in such a verdant forested location which was an absolute aromatic delight, especially in the early hours of the morning or late in the evening.

Holmsund was simply a woodland village and a small port for exporting timber. Umea was not much bigger but what really interested me was the number of bicycles. Everyone cycled and even the buses had racks both on their front and rear. The passengers temporarily hung their cycles on to the bus and retrieved them when they alighted.. I admired the cleanliness everywhere and the Swedes' love of bright colours. Typical bright woollen tammies with tassels and vivid colours overall, starting at their socks. It was a bright clean sparcely populated part of the world where they are born in the saddle and seem to pedal everywhere.

I happened to become friendly with a charming girl I found interested in learning to speak English. At the Mission for Seamen I became her tutor each evening and entertained her to great effect. Before our meetings she could not communicate other than by sign language and when we left two weeks later she was adept at completing exercises in English which I offered to correct.

It is amazing how much can be conveyed by sign language and some of the antics required to convey the meaning of thoughts were absolutely hilarious. The poor girl was in stitches and her cheek and tummy muscles ached after each of our laughter sessions. We had great fun and she had a wonderful sparkling personality which whisked days away as mere moments as we enjoyed ourselves.

We discharged that first load of timber at the Surrey Docks in the Thames. As you will realise, at that time coal was a regular cargo being exported from the UK. We loaded up with a full cargo of

Welsh Steam Coal at Barry and headed again for the Baltic. We anticipated the return cargo would be timber which would completely fill the ship and even be stacked up on deck to a height above fifteen feet. Rough weather might cause this to slip but that was just one of the risks which we accepted.

BLOWN UP

We had just entered the Baltic when alarm bells sounded. The ship was on fire! Spontaneous combustion of the coal meant that fire had started down in the holds and once alight the coal was proving that it could be a real menace. It was now burning fiercely and the fire was spreading.

I radioed ashore transmitting the urgency signal (XXX) which is sent in lieu of "SOS" because the ship was not in imminent danger of sinking but we had priority over all other communications except "Distress." This alerted everyone around and described our state of emergency. It enabled us to call for assistance as we then headed for Kotka in Finland. Our battle with the fire was hectic and it was all hands to the pumps as I radioed our predicament to the shore.

We desperately pumped water down holds numbers three and four endeavouring to quench the fire. Smoke was belching out and the fierce heat on deck was building up whilst the sides of the hull were seen to sizzle at sea level. The amount of sea we were pumping from various hoses into the ship built up until we began to list precariously. We could not afford to pump any more water into the holds. Tugs were requested to standby and firefighters were urgently summoned to assist. Because we presented a hazard we were not permitted to enter port. We had to stop just outside of Kotka where we were forced to anchor.

Listing dangerously, with so much water on board, no more could be risked, especially as it had not yet extinguished the fire. The captain at this stage decided that we should smother the fire and starve it of oxygen. The ventilators were hastily sealed with canvas hoods and the hatch covers replaced over the holds and firmly battened down to shut off all air to the fire. The hope was that this would starve the fire of air and smother it.

We had been struggling all afternoon and I was also involved in helping with the emergency but at this stage my services were no longer required. It was just after five o'clock in the evening so I went into the saloon for a meal. The steward was apologetic and because of the disruption he said that all he could manage was bacon and eggs. "Fine," I said, so he returned with rashers of bacon and two fried eggs.

I was seated alone in the saloon and I had just started to cut the bacon when suddenly whoooomph! There was an almighty, violent, explosion which felt as if the world was blowing apart. The blast was ear shattering. I thought that I was disintegrating as I felt myself surging upwards and becoming weightless. Up I went out of the chair into the air just aware that my feet were now dangling well above the top of the table. Instantly, I was flaying my arms trying to orientate to an upright position in my airborne state.

Immediately, I tried to paddle my legs like frenzy and seemed to be propelling myself forward, through the air, without even touching the deck. Frantically I shot out of the saloon and dashed over to the side of the ship. Maybe my intention was to jump into the sea but looking down, I saw great splashes were being caused by descending debris. Flying past me on its way down was a hatch cover which is a heavy baulk of timber like a railway sleeper. Had I jumped, I would have been struck by it or some of the other hulks of timber and the numerous flying missiles which were plummeting into the sea. Looking upwards, there were many more hatch covers and great chunks of coal. These large threatening objects had to be avoided. The darkened sky was a thick black cloud of coal dust and debris, thrown up out of the ship, with an explosive force that had everything leap upwards from the sea, including our ship. A multitude of materials was suspended overhead, with the lighter dust and smaller particles, having soared thousands of feet through the air and smoke. The blackened sky was under pinned by chunks of coal peppered everywhere in the heavens. Gazing upwards through the gloom, only a dark canopy of coal fragments could be seen.

Slowly, the heavier pieces of timber and larger blocks of coal turned and commenced their descent. Gradually, this had a grading effect on the debris. The smaller particles were still hovering in suspension five hundred feet above us in a black cloud. The dark smoke was still curling upwards and spreading outwards through the top. Starting to fall around me were mighty hunks of coal and these began to batter the ship, clanging down on the deck or splashing alongside into the sea.

Glancing upwards, I could still see huge dangerous pieces dropping at an alarming rate, so I dashed forward to the bow and gained an overhanging section of metal above me for protection. As I crouched down under it, I watched with amazement, as the sky slowly began to open up and clear. Thousands of fragments of coal were raining down into the sea as everything seemed to be dropping from out of the sky. Then, as the cloud thinned further, the ship was spattered with the smaller particles covering everything in a thickening layer of black dust. In torrents this heavy monsoon raged and showered on to our decks. Cloaked in the dark, one could hear and almost feel it all fall into the surrounding sea.

After a while things seemed to quieten down so I made my way back midships to assess the situation. The heart of the fire down in the hold was now exposed so that action could be taken to directly gain control. The fire fighting tug which had been summoned to assist could be seen steaming around our ship. Great jets of water were spewing out of its water canons. Fire hoses thrust water upwards from their nozzles some fifty feet into the air and outwards for one hundred feet forward. Unfortunately, all of this action fell at least one hundred yards short of the ship. No doubt the fire crew feared another explosion was imminent thus they circled around at a safe distance.

I realised that I still had not eaten so I cautiously made my way back to the saloon. Incredible, but there was no way that I could get in. The floor had been thrust upwards and formed into a great bulge. The doorway and deckhead had combined to shut off the space. It was impossible to get through the opening which had once been the doorway. Bending down, I looked into the saloon and there stuck to the ceiling, above where I had been seated, were two perfectly formed fried eggs. The physics of that achievement still baffles me. Likewise, the fact that I came out through that doorway as it was being transformed still amazes me.

Later, when I was dining ashore a conversation at the next table was overheard. The group was boasting about how near to disaster they were in the harbour. One chap was recounting how he had been thrown out of his bunk with the force of the explosion. Of course, that was about a mile away from the *ss.Canford,* which was anchored outside, so a smile creased my face. The occupants at the other table probably saw that I was amused. They called across, "Did you hear the explosion. Where were you at the big bang?" I had to be honest so I said, "I was aboard the *Canford!*"

Another amusing discovery was the method used to ask someone ashore, for the directions back to the docks. Nobody seemed to speak English and it was confusingly difficult, in sign language, to explain. However, when we mentioned the word "Canford," they would indicate with their hands the upward explosion and immediately direct us to the harbour.

FINLAND

We loaded successfully and returned to the UK.with a full cargo of timber. Later when we learned that we were bound again for "Kotka" in Finland, everyone began hoarding cigarettes, coffee and sugar. These items were like gold dust on the black market so enterprising marketeers on board, were set to make a killing. En route we were hailed by a small German fishing vessel just before entering the Kiel Canal. We stopped for a spot of ocean shopping as they pulled alongside. A large basket of herrings was hoisted on board our ship. Up came another basket, followed by yet another, brimming over with sea fresh herrings. On top of each basket was laid several good sized cod, one actually some four feet long which could have fetched an excellent price at home. In exchange, we lowered a couple of loaves, bottle of gin and some cigarettes. I thought that it was hard won black market exchange and that we could have been more generous to the Germans but our steward was in charge and at least we benefited with subsequent delicious meals. Never before had I enjoyed such perfection in fish. We were treated with over generous helpings because storage time in our ice box was limited. The sooner the fish could be eaten absolutely fresh the more they would be appreciated. Sentiments for which there were no dissenting voices.

Black market trading continued on arrival at Kotka and for a few pounds of coffee I obtained a splendid radio for my parents and another for my own use. In fact I was in constant demand to vet radios for members of our crew as they likewise picked up bargains from onshore. Perhaps it was the attraction of the black market goods which we had available which made our sailors susceptible to feminine wiles. On the otherhand, female Finns were said to be completely liberated and that doubtless was a truism. Certainly, there didn't seem to be any bachelor sailors amongst our numbers and 'breakfast for two' was the familiar call. The ladies in Finland undoubtedly formed close friendships because all bunks on the ship were allegedly singles.

We sailed back to the UK. and I was able to slip home from Grangemouth for a few days whilst unloading. On return to the ship Yxpila was announced as our destination for another load of timber. This is a small port only a few minutes away from Kotka in Finland so you can imagine that the pulses were sent racing at the thought of those wonderful nights and excellent breakfasts.

November 1947 started cold and grim so it followed that we had a stormy passage across the North Sea. A fierce Northerly gale kept us in one position for thirty hours. Despite our best endeavours to steam ahead, we covered only five miles one night and this relatively short passage in the North Sea became hazardous and protracted. I was glad that we were on a short haul because I managed very little sleep. Entering the "Skagerrak" with night approaching, I was in constant demand operating the Direction Finder due to the foul weather and later we were additionally endangered by fog. In fact, it was altogether a bad weather experience which even had members of our crew laid low with sea sickness. We rolled and pitched, making living aboard thoroughly wretched. For my part, although I was not actually sick, the task of peering over and listening to the Direction Finder throughout the night and early hours of the morning caused me to suffer severe heartburn. This was primarily as a consequence of the violent actions of the ship rolling around and the fasting period in the graveyard watch. (Twelve to four am.).

The first day we arrived in Yxpila it had started to snow. I was dressed in my uniform, sitting on the local bus on the short hop into town. Then, slowly I became aware of a stunning form, draped in a soft cuddly fur coat, which rippled past me as she made her way down the bus. As she stood on the platform about to alight I was simply mesmerised. If this was Finnish beauty I was an ardent fan. Then she looked down the bus and seemed to smile at a young uniformed sailor which made his pulse quicken its rhythm. She stepped off the bus and as she walked past she glanced up at me. I could sense strong vibes of affection so with no more hesitation, I surrendered. Quickly, I leapt out of my seat but the bus had already started to move so I had to await for the next stop before I could get off.

I raced back down the road to where I believed she had

disappeared into one of the houses but I did not know precisely its exact location. As I walked along I doubtless passed her house without realising which was the abode in question. The quest continued until I had eventually to turn around and retrace my steps. I crunched my way back in solitude through the fresh covering of snow which had fallen to a good six inches in depth. Then amazingly, up there ahead of me, again appeared the flowing apparition of that fur coat which I desperately longed to embrace. I imagined that she must have seen me walk past her house and had come out in response to my mental waves of anguish.

I quickened my stride until I was almost walking alongside and able to return the smile in her eyes. She flirted with a shrug of her shoulders which set the fur coat quivering in ripples down her back.. The collogue was electrifying and enticed me as with her culminating gesture she said, "Kalte!" Now I didn't think so at the time but my German teacher at school was correct when he said that it was useful to have a 'working' knowledge of this language. I remembered that 'Kalte' meant 'cold.' Immediately, I put my arm across the back of that gorgeous soft fur coat and slipping my arm around her waist I said, "Eine Kalte aber zwei nicht Kalte!" (One cold but two not cold). The teacher would have been proud of me because what I remembered of the language was 'working!' She showed me the sights of town and by way of thanks I offered her hospitality, "Chez Canford."

Ladies wear fur coats because they are glamorous and the menfolks agree that they look soft, sensual and sexy. These initial attractions do not last and are insufficient for a meeting of minds and that is necessary if Cupid is to turn up the heat in a relationship. My next assignment enabled Cupid to kindle his fire which soon flamed to furnace intensity. Little wonder, because she was quite different and absolutely entrancing. She was an accomplished musician and despite my modest musical attunement our compatability mushroomed into a harmonious relationship. In fact our melody intensified until I was reminded of the passion in that tune "Night and Day." Such a hauntingly beautiful longing which even the   surrounding snow was powerless to cool.

It was sad to experience in life, that the greater the heights of pleasure reached, the more devastating would be the consequential fall. "The Leavin" on this occasion had an especial poignancy. The night on which we sailed out of the harbour she was due to perform on Helsinki radio. I was glued to my radio until I heard her voice announce her special fan's request number. Then her voice and guitar music drifted across the air waves and out over the Baltic Sea. Not surprisingly, her voice trembled slightly as I heard her sing my name. Now that was "The Leavin" that dampened even Cupid's eyes.

It would be next spring before we could again visit Baltic waters because of the big freeze. Ours was the last ship able to load timber and escape. We were actually frozen up in the harbour and an ice-breaking vessel had to attack the ice to enable us to break free.

MEDITERRANEAN
When we arrived back in West Hartlepool the dockers started to unload. It took them three weeks but when we sailed over to Antwerp they were able to load us in only three days. That was the comparable working rates of dockers in both countries. Unfortunately, we lost our cargo which was to be picked up at Lisbon. Because of the delay at West Hartlepool, our cargo was placed with another ship, so we proceeded straight to Gibraltar and then to Kalamata in Greece.

JEWS & ARABS IN CONFLICT
Next stop was Haifa where we were helping with the withdrawal of British army stores as they prepared to leave Palestine. During World War Two the Jews were largely supportive of our efforts. At the end of the war, the 'Stern Gang,' a Jewish terrorist organisation, fought British and Arabs alike to make Palestine a Jewish state. The King David Hotel, used by the British in Jerusalem, was blown up with nearly one hundred deaths. The ship, 'Exodus',

in 1947 was carrying 4,500 Jews emigrating from America to Palestine but it was forbidden to land them because of the tremendous influx of Jews into Palestine. We were regarded as anti-Semitic, but in our administration of Palestine, we wished to be fair to both Arabs and Jews. British restrictions of Jewish immigration provoked a campaign of bombing and shooting by Jewish extremist groups.

We referred the matter to the United Nations in 1947 and they wished to partition the country into Arab and Jewish States. This was rejected by the Arabs who renewed their attacks on the invading Jews. We ventured into this melee and when in Haifa, bombing, and shots being fired ashore, continued throughout both night and day. Never a day passed without a nearby building being blown up or someone being shot in sight of our ship. In fact one bullet whizzed on board and struck one of our crew.

British Palestine Police and our Armed Forces were preparing to withdraw, reluctant to have any further involvement in peace-keeping. As we steadily withdrew, the Arabs and Jews were preparing for confrontation because the Arabs would not accept the invading Jews and their attempt to create of a new State of Israel.

After our withdrawal in May 1948 the Jews fought in battle with Arabs involving Egypt, Iraq, Lebanon and Syria. The Jews were the victors, the exception was Jordan, whose King seized the West Bank of the River Jordan and East of Jerusalem, ostensibly for the Arabs, but more especially for Jordan. The Palestine Arabs were left without any state. We arrived February 1948 but we were forbidden to go ashore in Haifa. When we went to Egypt we were not permitted ashore supposedly because we came from Palestine and had to be in quarantine but this decision was political. Thus, without shore leave either at Haifa or Alexandria, the days on board ship as we lay in Haifa Bay were mounting up. It was sixty-three days since I had trod on dry land.

FACING THE FIRING SQUAD

Finally, well it was almost! The period was when the Israeli Arab conflict in Haifa and Palestine was at its height. Britain was in this "no win" situation and we were involved assisting to remove stores and equipment. 100.000 British troops were still stationed in Palestine. We were awaiting our turn to go alongside in Haifa, but were becoming quite frustrated, as we languished at anchor in Haifa Bay. Then one day, the Captain suggested we launch the ship's lifeboat and take a spin over to Acre which is an Arab town at the northern end of Haifa Bay. Perhaps if we did not venture ashore at least we could have a swim in the bay. "Would I like to come along?" Why not, any excuse to go boating, my speciality!

It was a beautiful sunny day, as might be expected in the Mediterranean, and we set off to Acre about ten miles across the bay. On approach, Acre loomed into view like a painting from "The Arabian Nights." The mosques and minarets of Acre's Old City overlook its harbour. The tall minarets and the dome of the Grand Mosque created an impressive Arabic silhouette. Seaward, the town is protected by a long high fortress wall with turrets, firing slits and a castellated top. It was a formidable fortified port and definitely unlike a holiday beach. Darting heads appeared at various points along the top of the fortifying wall. We were being watched and there was an air of foreboding and furtiveness distinctly evident even to our dull imaginations.

In hushed silence, we slid forwards to a low landing stage. The sun was dazzling and reflected in bright flashes from the glassy surface of the water. Carefully, I slowed down the engine and we rippled smoothly to halt alongside the stage. I hesitated before shutting off the engine but my companions were already scrambling out and it seemed appropriate to stop engine and tie up. A group of Arab guards stood nearbye and watched with a mixture of menace and amazement.

Our captain said that he and the chief steward would go take a look-see and then report, if we didn't mind waiting for a moment or two. They disappeared through two high iron gates which were swung between a pair of huge turreted towers. There was an area of about thirty yards across the forecourt from our boat to the high fortifying wall and the gates. We had tied up against the stone landing stage.

The guards armed with their rifles were becoming agitated. They looked like soldiers from the foreign legion with capes down the back of their necks. A leader appeared and approached our Third Mate. "You identity card?" he demanded. Whereupon, the Third Mate fumbled in the rear pocket of his shorts and produced the document.

Next the Second Mate was challenged, "You identity card?" He shrugged his shoulders and tried to explain that he hadn't brought it with him but he was English and Second Mate off the British ship "Canford."You didn't need to understand Arabic to realise the guard's command rasped out, **"Stand over there. Back against the wall!"**

It was now the turn of the Chief Engineer to be questioned. "You identity card?" The Chief, with his most charming smile explained that he had just come along with the captain and that he was Chief Engineer from that British ship out there in the bay. It was obvious that the guard didn't accept his answer and directed him to get over there with his back against the wall. "Steady on there," said our Chief. "I have told you who I am" he prevaricated. Whereupon, the guard withdrew his bayonet and fixed it on his rifle. "Ouch! that hurt," said the Chief as the guard prodded him with the bayonet and he backed off to the wall as the guard prodded him rather viciously, once more, to be sure.

Cheers went up from the crowd of onlookers now gathering along the top of the wall and peering down at the scene. Meantime, I was in the boat coiling a rope with my head down trying to be invisible or at the very least nonchalant. Not any more, because the guard swung round and said, **"You Jew?!"** emphatically, I said, **"No!"** and despite my firm negative reply, I was also thrust into the position against the wall. I was beginning to think that we should not have come and that identity papers of any sort might have been helpful.

There was no sign of the captain or our chief steward. As we three huddled together, someone murmured the obvious that it seemed we were going to be shot. Some children had slipped through the gates and were being ushered back out of sight. The crowd behind us and those leaning over the wall were now chanting, **"Jehudi! Jehudi!"** The strutting guards looked confident, egged on by the admiring crowd who were baying for blood yelling encouragement on all sides

The leading guard approached us and prodding each of us with his bayonet, forced us to separate and shouted commands to effectively line us up against the wall. As it was evident that we were going to be shot I had manouvered myself into the middle. I figured that when the first shot was fired, the victim would be on the right or left of me depending upon whether or not the marksman was right or left-handed. He would first shoot the man on the right or left before the one in the middle. Beyond that I wrestled with my thoughts because there seemed nowhere to go. Behind us was that great high wall with the baying crowd becoming increasingly vociferous with vicious intent. What should I do?

I could make a dash for the boat but it was just too far to escape without receiving a bullet. It would take too long to escape that way. At the best I would be shot in the back. Even if I reached the water and plunged in to swim away I would still be an easy target. It seemed that there was no way out and no escape possible. Whilst I was working out what could be done, the guard turned with his back towards us and started to take twenty paces forward. He halted and did an about turn to face us. He pulled back the bolt of his rifle and the gun was now primed ready to shoot. He raised his rifle and was taking aim, so now was the time for action. My mind was made up. After the first shot I would dash forward and grab the rifle with the hope of getting it away in the boat.

The rifle was raised, awaiting the command to fire. I focussed on the end of the rifle, seeing just a little round hole. I scratched my breast bone with my finger. I could already feel the hole in my chest. Something flashed out from my left. It was the plump figure of a man running forward to the guard gesticulating with his arms flaying in the air. He caught hold of the rifle pushing the gun down. The guard struggled to raise it once more and pointed it in our direction. Yet again it was forced down and this time the other guards joined in the squabble. Meanwhile the cries of **"Jehudi! Jehudi!"** (Jew! Jew!) rang out from the ever increasing hostile crowd who were obviously baying for our blood.

The pannicking guards seemed to quieten down somewhat as this plump fellow shouted ferociously at them. They became more subdued as he seemed to convince them that we were indeed bona fide British seamen and not Jewish immigrants. Then we were ordered to get into the boat and told to wait offshore until the signal to return. We willingly did so, motoring a good distance out before daring to hover around. Then, seeing the signal, somewhat dubiously edged back in towards that fateful landing stage. All our eyes were searching to see if the captain was there. Yes, he was present all right together with the steward. We touched alongside. They hopped into the boat and we were off full throttle!

It appeared that the captain and steward were at first imprisoned in a dungeon at the base of one of the stone towers. After some arguing, the captain with the aid of his identity card convinced the soldiers that he had come ashore to buy provisions but not from Haifa because he was more in favour of the Arabs and had come to

Acre. On this account, he was loaned an Arab guard escort to proceed to the market to shop for the goods required.

I think it must have been at that stage we were granted our new lease of life. The captain suggested that the stout fellow should return to the boat to ensure that we were safe and awaiting the captain's return. The captain and his escort proceeded towards the market to select provisions but they were being jostled by an ever growing crowd. The situation became increasingly hostile with the crowd shouting "Jehudi, Jehudi!" Things became decidedly menacing and the guard, with his rifle pointing into the crowds could easily have been overwhelmed. He was beginning himself to show signs of fear.

The captain indicated that they should go back to the gaol. He then explained that he would return tomorrow to collect the stores. This settled, he was brought back to the landing stage. The stout merchant entrepreneur who helped recover the situation no doubt anticipated that there would be a large sum of money involved in such a transaction. As it happened, the following day stores finally arrived for the ship.

The Naval authorities learned of our escapade and reinforced the order that Acre was strictly out of bounds. They also emphasised that we were indeed fortunate to have survived. When we did eventually go alongside in Haifa to load army stores I was approached by some soldiers with the request to mend their radio. I had a look at the receiver and suggested where the fault lay but explained that I did not have the replacement spares required to put it in order. Whereupon, other defunct radios appeared and I was told to cannibalise them and fix what was possible. I had a wonderful time and of course liberated a communication receiver for my own personal use. I also obtained an army orientating compass together with all the fruit and cream that could possibly be absorbed by my body.

Due to lack of shore leave and unable to do any shopping the bo-sun had run out of batteries for his radio. I decided to convert it to run off the ship's main electric supply. I didn't have spares to construct a small compact eliminator but with a combination of various lamps in lieu of resistances to achieve the voltage drops, I rigged up his converted mains radio. Later, when I had salvaged chokes, condensers and transformers he declined an updated system. He was delighted to have a maze of wires condensers and flickering lamps of various sizes which looked remarkably scientific. He was amusingly referred to as 'Faraday' with his power station and he had no wish to diminish his reputation.

Reflecting upon wizardry, the best magician I ever encountered was the "Gillie Gillie Man" in Alexandria. I was sceptical of his powers until he convinced me by pulling chickens out of my pockets, pants and ears. From anywhere he could extract a live chicken. I foolishly bet that he couldn't take a coin out of my tightly closed hand. He did so, with of course, the loss of my coin. Still it was worth it and good value entertainment.

We continued the evacuation of Palestine with round trips to Malta, Tripoli, Benghazi, Tel-Aviv, Famagusta, Port Said, Piraeus, Salonica, Alexandria and Haifa. Malta featured in our run to these Mediterranean ports at which we discharged the army stores retrieved from Palestine. Lingering still could be seen the aftermath and heroism of the Maltese Islanders who were virtually bombed and starved almost to the point of surrender. But in August 1942 they were relieved by "Operation Pedestal." This was the Merchant Navy convoy, most heavily defended and most heavily attacked, during the war in the Mediterranean.

OPERATION PEDESTAL
Fifty-nine Royal Navy vessels escorted **fourteen Merchant Navy ships** to enable them to win through with essential provisions for the starving and exhausted Maltese. Commendable efforts on the part of Captain Rodger Hill of HMS."Ledbury" helped to rescue

forty-five merchant seamen from the blazing inferno of what remained of their ship, the bombed "Waimarama." He said that on this occasion he was determined to stay and assist the merchant ships and thus to redeem his conduct and the disgrace he felt at leaving them on convoy PQ17.

In "Operation Pedestal" it was a battle ferociously fought with only **five magnificent merchant ships** victoriously surviving in the convoy and limping into the Maltese harbour at Valetta. This included the remarkable survival of the legendary tanker the *mv.Ohio* which had been repeatedly bombed and was at one point a blazing inferno yet it managed to crawl into Malta.

Due to the arrival of the relief food supplies, ammunition and fuel, Malta did not have to surrender. Still evident everywhere was the destruction wrought by months of suffering from the heaviest bombing. Stricken ships sunk in Grand Harbour, Streets and buildings reduced to rubble. Utter devastation everywhere brought back forcibly those memories of heroism.

EXODUS

Fortunately, just before we left Haifa, I watched the final exodus of Palestine with Commissioner Cunningham making his way out of the harbour to the cruiser "Euralysis." The timing was excellent and as his launch raced out to the cruiser in Haifa Bay, groups of four RAF. planes came out of the sky and dipped low over his launch. Simultaneously, the cruiser fired its gun salute and thus ended our administration of Palestine.

At Port Said I used to spend Sundays up on monkey island (flat deck area on top of the ship's bridge) with binoculars watching the yacht races. The streamlined hulls of these elegant craft seemed to sail so gracefully in the perfect weather conditions. The sky was bright blue, the sea a magnificent aquamarine and the winds had that landward breeze of the tropics. I was entranced with the peace and pleasure of this sport and I knew that I could not delay much longer becoming involved. This experience stirred nostalgic memories of sailing on the Clyde in the summer regattas. I had recently enjoyed repairing radios and together, these thoughts inspired me to answer an advert for a radio mechanic in the U.K. My application for the job was accepted so I swallowed the anchor.

14

DIRTY BRITISH COASTER

After spending three years ashore, I sailed as Sparks on my last ship the **SS.LESTO.** The name, I believe, in musical terms translates "with less pace, slow and easy." Musicians might correctly prefer the spelling "Lento." My two young nieces on the otherhand
thought it most appropriate to paint the name "Lesto" on the shell of the tortoise which I gave them. Whatever the spelling the tempo perfectly suited my requirements since I was on vacation.

Between first and second year studies I went back to sea as the lucrative way to replenish dwindling reserves. I could not obtain a grant because Merchant Navy personnel were not regarded as ex Servicemen. Thus, I had to pay for my education and also support myself.

The fable of *the tortoise and the hare* confirms the virtue of constancy. *Lesto* confirmed my belief that an ambition in life, if nurtured, will unquestionably be achieved. Thus it was a fitting conclusion to sail between Tyne and Thames on this *Dirty British Coaster* complete *with her salt caked smoke stack.*

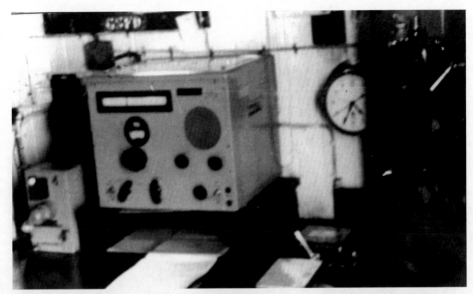

Radio Room ss.Lesto.Final voyage on vacation from studies.

SS.LESTO.BUILT 1919.1,500 Grt. Tyne/Thames collier.
Dirty British Coaster with her Salt Caked Smokestack.

The Author as 1st R/O.

Dear Robert

A splendid book, a truly readable book, which I couldn't put down. Which a landlubber was enlightend by a lot of nautacal terms.
Now follows a little post script.

Hallowed river, most gracious trees, chapel beyond compare
Here be gentlemen sick of the seas take them into your care.
Far have they come, much have they braved, give them their hour of play.
While the hidden things their hands have saved work for them day by day
Far have they steamed and much have they known, and most they would fain forget.
But now they are come to their joyous own with all the world in their debt.

Thanks
Jack

A splendid job! I thoroughly enjoyed every page.

Norman S.

-oOo-

Agreed - I honestly didn't put it down. Fascinating, and the description of the Atlantic Storm - awe inspiring.

Bob G.

-oOo-

As an 'indifferent' female to the Seaman's cause, I found this book surprisingly readable, and in parts, most absorbing.

Written from the heart, Robert has successfully conveyed to me, the stark day to day realities of the Seaman's life during the war.

With sensitive touches of humour, sadness and acceptance of one's own fate, he roused my interest and nurtured it throughout the book.

Janice H.

-oOo-